MW00896873

Learning to Walk

Joe Henderson

How walk breaks added miles to
my runs and years to my running

Learning to Walk

How walking added miles
to my runs and years
to my running

By Joe Henderson in 2015

Cover photo from Victoria Half-Marathon

Joe Henderson was for more than 30 years a columnist and editor at *Runner's World* magazine, and he has published more than 30 books. He's a veteran of more than 700 races, from sprints to ultras. He coaches a local marathon/half-marathon team, and taught running classes at the University of Oregon for 18 years. His columns appear on Facebook as Joe Henderson's Writings.

This and many more books by the author are available in print and as ebooks from Amazon.com. The titles:

Going Far: Reflecting on the years when running grew up, and a writing career took off.

Home Runs: Moving on and settling down in the post-peak years.

Joe's Team: How training plans work when the writer becomes the coach.

Learning to Walk: How walk breaks added miles to my runs and years to my running.

Long Run Solution: What I like best about running, and do most as a runner.

Long Slow Distance: The humane way to train.

Miles to Go: Complete set of columns for Marathon & Beyond, *2004 to 2011.*

Pacesetters: Runners who informed me best and inspired me most.

Run Right Now: What a half-century of running has taught.

Run Right Now Training Log: Set goals, record your progress, and take your running to the next level. (Not available as an e-book.)

See How We Run: Best writings from 25 years of Running Commentary.

Starting Lines: Early efforts of a writing runner, and where they led.

This Runner's World: Complete set of "Joe Henderson's Journal" columns from that magazine, 1987 to 2004.

Contents

Dedicated to Ernst van Aaken, who introduced me to walking for runners long before I was ready to listen... to Ken Crutchlow, my first convincer... to Tom Osler, who refined the practice... and to Jeff Galloway, who made it acceptable.

Introduction: Walking Lessons

(2015) WALKING LESSONS? You might think these are as unnecessary as eating or breathing lessons. Isn't walking a skill we learn around the age of one, pretty much master by two and then never forget?

Not really. Children don't suddenly stand up and walk. Their first steps are lunging runs into the arms of waiting parents. They don't slow down much until their teenaged years, then soon get a driver's license and thereafter limit their walking to crossing parking lots or trekking home when the car breaks down.

A few of us keep running after learning to drive. I was among those lucky ones that way. However, more than 20 years passed between my first formal race and my return to walking. I took that long to adopt walk breaks as good and necessary additions to what remains today a running-centered routine.

As my years add up, the miles slow down. But I'm still a runner, in practice as well as at heart. You don't stop being one just because the pace and distance ease down.

My running dates from my first unsteady steps into racing on April Fools Day 1958 and continues at an age when I could be the grandfather of that kid who ran then. I've raced hundreds of times, from sprints to ultras. I've finished marathons in six decades – from my 20s to 70s.

I made a career of writing articles and books about running. I spoke about the sport before any group that would listen. Now I teach running classes at a university and coach teams of marathoners.

Running has set the course of my life. I still run, and think, act and work like a runner.

That said, I quickly admit that today I'm half the runner I was at half this age. That's almost numerically true. My distances are about half as long, my pace half as fast.

I also freely confess that less than half of the "run" time nowadays is spent running. Walks come often, and some days pure walks replace runs. Pure runs are as rare as lunar eclipses.

This confession will amuse, annoy, alarm or anger purist runners, but not inspire them to walk. I felt the same way myself once.

While training for track, I made it a point of pride never to walk for recovery between hard intervals but to shuffle at little more than walking pace. I jogged in small circles while waiting impatiently for stoplights to go green.

I thought "walk" was a shameful word, if not an epithet. Walking was for people who wouldn't run at all and for ex-runners who couldn't run anymore. Real runners *ran*.

My thinking changed completely, but only slowly. This book recounts how I gradually and sometimes grudgingly made peace with walking, and why I now praise and promote its beauties and benefits.

Walking hasn't replaced my running but has added to it. Walk breaks, the simplest and best type of cross-training, have extended my life as a runner. I happily stop to walk if it keeps me running longer – if not in miles, then in years.

1. Before Walking

(1969) THE 1960S CHANGED me more dramatically than any other decade. Little of this had to do with the country's tumult in those times (though I did serve peripherally, as a reservist, in the wartime Army while protesting only at the voting booth). Most of my changes came simply from passing between ages 16 and 26, when we all search for what we want to do with the rest of our life. I grew up, that is, and assumed my adult shape.

When the sixties dawned, I was a high school junior living in a tiny Iowa town. Where I'd go next hadn't yet come into focus. I had my dreams and schemes, but no plans beyond running each mile race faster than the last while trying to win a college scholarship somewhere as a runner.

When the sixties closed, I lived in an idyllic suburb of San Francisco. I worked for the magazine that had first fed my running fantasies, *Track & Field News*. My writing hands had taken me where my running legs couldn't, to the 1968 Olympics in Mexico City. I'd published my first book in 1969, and had plans for the second. I would start at new job, at *Runner's World*, on the first business day of the next decade. I would first date my wife-to-be that same week.

"My" decade saw my mile time drop by more than 20 seconds, then climb by almost 40 from the fastest to the latest race. In those years my longest race jumped from two-tenths less than two miles to two-tenths more than 26. Both my mile and marathon PRs became permanent, as did all other important records.

My training went from mostly fast to all slow. The switch came in 1966 while training for my first marathon (and *only* one, according to the original plan). The slowdown changed my approach to running more dramatically than any move made before or since. I described it a slim book titled *Long Slow Distance: The Humane Way to Train*.

Amid all these changes, there was one constant. I never did any voluntary walking. Oh sure, at times I *had* to walk when marathon distance and pace left no choice. But I wrote off those walks as failures of body or will. I thought walking had nothing good to offer a runner like me.

COMING ATTRACTIONS

The 1960s held hints of future walking possibilities. At the time I batted them away repeatedly as irrelevant to me. In order of appearance these were:

1. *Ernst van Aaken*, a German medical doctor and coach, wrote in a 1960 issue of *Track Technique* magazine how his runners, fastest to slowest, mixed]walk breaks into their runs. This wasn't traditional interval training, used to gain speed. Van Aaken's runners extended the practice to their endurance runs.

Walking seemed unnecessary when I already could run pretty far without taking any breaks. More attractive to me was advice from Arthur Lydiard from New Zealand, featured in a 1961 *Track Technique* issue. Lydiard's distance-based training didn't include walking.

The New Zealander's runners won Olympic medals in 1960. I knew about them but only later would notice van

Aaken-coached Harald Norpoth placing second in the 5000 at the 1964 Games.

2. *Bill Bowerman* became Lydiard's disciple and then a missionary himself after a 1962 visit to New Zealand. Lydiard had convinced thousands of his countrymen to run for their health. Bowerman, never before a distance runner, joined some of them. His fitness improved dramatically in just a few weeks.

He was as convincing back home in Oregon as Lydiard had been in his hometown and then his country. Bowerman attracted throngs of converts in Eugene. He couldn't coach each one individually, so with a local doctor he wrote simple advice and sample schedules.

This pamphlet, picked up by a national publisher in 1966 as a book titled *Jogging*, became the first big seller on the subject. It preached that mixing walking with running is the safest and best way to start.

3. *Kenneth Cooper, M.D.,* outdid Bowerman in book sales – by a bunch. Dr. Cooper's *Aerobics* made national best-seller lists in 1968. It became the most influential exercise book ever written.

Cooper offered running as one aerobic exercise among many (bicycling and swimming also getting high marks even in those pre-triathlon times). Running happened to be his own favorite as a longtime runner, but he also liked its efficiency: the most aerobic gain in the least activity time.

Like Bowerman, Cooper knew that nonstop runs weren't safe at first. So he recommended advancing through stages of pure walk, to walk/run, to run/walk, to run only.

SIXTIES SLOWDOWN

All of this evidence and more should have softened my views toward walking. The "more" was quite personal.

By the mid-1960s my running had slowed to a pace that runners of that time considered little more than a walk. Gone was all speed training, and with it any reason to take pseudo-walks (by dead-stopping for a few minutes between fast segments or jogging slower than walking pace). Gone too were hard time-trials (now known as "tempo runs") and hill repeats.

The only time I ran fast was in races, where it counted. Otherwise the pace was relaxed, which may have been why this practice worked for me; I recovered better, stayed healthier and felt more ready to race than when I'd "raced" most of the training.

Running this way, I PRed at all distances 5K and above. On marathon training I came within 10 seconds of the one-mile time I'd run while training as a miler.

This approach came to be known as "long slow distance." It led to the book with that title, published in 1969.

My message, that training could be better slower, was more radical for those speed-obsessed times than my recommending walk breaks would be later. Before, my interval sessions had averaged sub-five-minute pace. After the great slowdown, each mile of a long run took about three minutes longer.

Moving from steady runs to run/walk would have added only a minute per mile to that pace. But I still wasn't nearly ready to try walking.

I still stopped for nothing short of an insurmountable wall or an imminent collapse. I still drank without breaking stride. I still ran in place at stoplights, as if lightning would strike me dead if I walked a step.

I reached the height of anti-walking absurdity while driving. I circled parking lots, waiting for a spot to open nearest the store. I could run 26 miles without stopping but wouldn't walk an extra 26 yards.

My resistance to walking was strong as the sixties ended. It was soon to weaken, then break for good.

LONGER, EASIER

The *Long Slow Distance* book never mentioned walking. But hints of what was to come already lay between these lines from *LSD's* introduction, written in 1969:

Everything we've been led to believe about distance training points to one hard and fast principle: training has to be hard and fast. Habitually skeptical runners, brought up as we all are believing in this principle, aren't easily convinced there's a more pleasant alternative.

If he hadn't lived through the experience, Amby Burfoot might have laughed off the suggestion that he could average 5:04 miles in a marathon after averaging two minutes slower on training runs. Ed Winrow would have questioned the wisdom, too, of anyone telling him he could go two miles in 8:55 without going much faster per *mile* in practice. Bob Deines, Tom Osler and Jeff Kroot would have doubted their chances of improving their marathons by an hour... with slower training.

It doesn't make sense. But it has worked that way for them. As much as this idea of going rather long, rather slowly conflicts with present training conventions, there's nothing really radical or even new about this approach. It's

11

the height of conservatism and is as old as the instincts we've inherited from our ancient ancestors.

Bob Carman, a longtime distance student and recent convert to the relaxed (in pace, that is; he goes as long as 50 miles in individual runs) form of training, pointed out to me after my original LSD article appeared in *Distance Running News* that Arthur Newton was using and recommending the same more than 40 years earlier.

Newton was the world's greatest ultra-distance man in his day — a day when such races were in vogue. Even though the marathon was his minimum distance, he was running around 2:40 in an era when that time would place well in the Olympics.

Newton wrote in his book, *Races and Training*, "Two primary considerations are essential: (1) You must practice as frequently as you possibly can, and (2) you must never permit yourself to approach real exhaustion, must never become badly tired. So long as you stick to these two, you will continuously progress. The less closely you adhere, the longer it will take you to get thoroughly fit."

The voice from a half-century ago continues, "I am convinced that it doesn't help you in any way at any time to practice sheer speed, although that is what practically every athlete has been taught to do and does. Actual racing in running, or all-out exertion in any other form of sport, should be confined solely to the competition for which you are training, and such events will be all the better if they are few and far between compared with what goes on nowadays.

"Every [one] of us, like every other animal, is born with all the speed he is likely to require. It has been built up through all the countless centuries of our evolution. Just consider wild animals, which on the whole are certainly much healthier than the average modern man. They run plenty, but never at any time for all they are worth unless obliged to by absolute fear. Even then it is only being scared stiff that will make them extend to their utmost.

"So if you take this nature lesson to heart, you will know that sheer racing should be kept within distinctly restricted limits. Set about running, then, to run in an easy and serene manner, knowing that once learned — and even during the learning — you can thoroughly enjoy every bit of the exercise."

2. Longest Days

(1971) IN THOUSANDS of pages of writing spread across a half-century I've said precious little about ultrarunning. That's because my history beyond the marathon is as brief and incomplete as it is ancient.

My ultra "career" lasted but 19 months, from spring 1970 to fall 1971. I entered five ultras, dropped out of four and completed only the shortest of them. But this isn't to say I failed miserably at ultras.

I recall here my single success and what first appeared to be my greatest failure, at least for number of miles left unfinished. Later I realized there are no bad experiences if they teach good lessons.

One of the best races I ever ran, at any long distance, was a baby ultra just six miles longer than a marathon. No surprise that it also was the only one I went into well prepared.

Preparation began with a 30-mile training run of sorts, when I stopped at that point of a 50-mile race in late 1970. Then, a month later, came another 30 (my longest-ever true training run). A month after that I ran a marathon race (more training-in-disguise).

This led to a 32-mile race from Santa Rosa, California, to Petaluma and back in early 1971. Today's ultra runners who climb mountains on trails might call this race of little more than a 50K on flat roads "just a slightly long marathon." It seemed plenty long to me, thank you, as I passed the marathon checkpoint at seven-minute pace with almost another 10K to go.

The pace actually picked up a bit in those extra miles. I would have taken more pride in my finish that day if I'd known it wouldn't be the first of many in ultras. It would be the one and only.

STOP AND GO LONGER

Ken Crutchlow was not a runner. He told me so himself in a 1971 interview for *Runner's World*. Yet this 27-year-old, who called London home while spending precious little time there, accidently had found himself doing plenty of running in recent months.

With no training to back him up, in quick succession he: (1) crossed Death Valley, in 130-degree midday heat, the 130-mile trek taking 57 hours; (2) traveled from Los Angeles to San Francisco, 550 miles by his route, in 10 days; (3) relayed with a partner across California, 280 miles including a climb to 7000 feet of elevation, in 67 hours.

"This running started totally by accident," Ken recalled. "I hadn't done any since 1965, when I would run about eight miles a week with my mates from a rowing club – to become a better oarsman. In 1970 my friend John Fairfax had rowed across the Atlantic by himself. He made the remark, 'Though I walk through the valley of death, I'll fear no evil, because I'm the meanest SOB in the valley.'

"I repeated it later and mixed it up a bit by saying, 'Though I walk through Death Valley.' John told me, 'You could never walk through Death Valley.' I'm never one to pass up a challenge, so I said, 'Walk it, hell; I'll *run* it!' And off I went to California."

Of this run through the hottest U.S. desert, Ken said, "I had no idea of pace or what I should do. I started out wearing my pin-striped suit and bowler hat. I got rid of the suit plenty quick, but I always wore my bowler. I never go without my bowler.

"I started out running in two-mile bursts, with a five-minute rest between them. But as the days went by, my runs got shorter and my rests longer. At one point I was down to covering one mile in an hour."

Surprisingly for one with so little running background, his worst troubles came early in the run when he picked up severe blisters. But then he seemed to grow stronger toward the end, 2½ days later.

After 50-odd hours with little food ("I was drinking five gallons of liquid a day, but so were the non-runners accompanying me in the car"), he hot-footed the last 20 miles in four hours. "I felt I'd die all the time," he said, "and I was in a hurry to get the damn thing over with."

As our interview ended, I asked if he plans further endurance tests – knowing full well that he might set out to run across the United States next week or might already have run his last step. "Oh," he said, " I don't plan these things. That's half the fun, going into them unprepared. Unlike marathoners who train every day, I don't know my capabilities. I'm always surprising myself with what I'm able to do."

This conversation prompted me to see how far I could run by stopping to rest .

LESSONS FROM "FAILURE"

Runners place great, and sometimes undeserved, faith in the power of numbers. We once thought, for instance, that reaching 100 miles in a single week was vastly superior to stopping at 99. A runner might sneak out at 10 minutes to midnight on a week's last day to go the extra mile, which does nothing more for the body but lifts the spirits.

I never did anything so silly because I never came close enough to 100 miles to try. My best training week ended in the 80s. But if you let me include racing in the total, I did nudge into triple digits – once.

That week in 1971 began with a marathon, a full effort that ended up being my second fastest (and within 37 seconds of my PR). The weekday recovery runs totaled 20 miles, then the weekend brought another race. It would lift my Sunday to Saturday mileage to at least 105 – or higher, depending on whether or not you count the wee hours of the second Sunday morning as a continuation of Saturday night.

If not for Ken Crutchlow, I never would have believed it possible to go so far, so soon after a marathon. The British adventurer inspired me to try breaking a long run into segments for the first time.

Talking with Ken after he'd covered 550 miles in 10 days, I asked how he had trained for this. "Oh, I did no training," he said. "Where's the sport in that? I wanted to see how far I could go without any specific preparation."

So how could he possibly go 50-plus miles, day after day? "I ran a few miles, then rested a bit, then ran again," he told me. "It took the whole bloody day to reach my quota, but I eventually got there."

What was good enough for the untrained Crutchlow seemed good enough for mildly trained me. The weekend after my 2:50 marathon I entered a 100-mile race in Rocklin, California, to test his technique. My longest run ever had been 35 miles, so my distance limit shouldn't have been much longer than that. But Ken had convinced me to try for more – much more – by going and stopping repeatedly.

I began by running five miles at a time, two laps of this course, then taking a few minutes' break. These weren't walk breaks between running segments. They were *rest* breaks, with runs resuming exactly where they'd left off. I wanted to say I'd *run* the full distance, even if I'd called timeouts.

This practice brought jibes from fellow runners. "You're quitting already?" asked one early in the race. "With 95 miles to go?"

I carried on with five miles at a time through 50, then dropped to 2½ miles while lingering longer than before during rest breaks. Midnight passed. The house lights along the route flickered out.

Four other runners remained on the course somewhere, but I hadn't seen any of them for hours. I had never felt so alone. Nothing I'd ever done in running seemed quite so senseless as running these laps by myself in the darkness after I'd already run so many.

A lone official stood, recording laps, in a golf course parking lot that marked the start and end of each lap. I sat down there for my break after the 70th mile and couldn't get back up. The thought of going on was too depressing. I mumbled to the scorer, "That's it for me. Write 'DNF' [did not finish] on your sheet."

Another runner, Peter Mattei, sprawled in the back of his station wagon. He was only resting, not dropping out. "What do you mean you're quitting?" said Peter. "You can't stop now. You only have 30 miles to go."

He was serious. Compared to the 70 miles we'd traveled, another 30 didn't sound like much. But it was almost as far as I'd ever gone before this day. It was six to seven more hours at a time when I couldn't face six or seven more minutes.

By dropping out, I failed. But in other ways this effort was, if not a success, at least a great… what? "Revelation" is too strong a word here, because of it sounds too religious. I wasn't yet ready to worship at the altar of walk breaks, but my stop-breaks did reveal three surprising compensations for my DNF:

1. *Farther*. My longest distance without taking intentional breaks had been 35 miles. That had come in the failed three-day "100," when I'd set a distance PR the first day but couldn't answer the bell the next morning. Here I went exactly twice that far, faster and easier.

2. *Faster*. The 70 miles took more than 14 hours and, with stops, averaged more than 12 minutes per mile (which doesn't sound nearly as slow now as it did then). But the running pace, with break time subtracted, dropped to 8:13s. That compared favorably with the 6:30s of my marathon the week before – for more than 2½ times that distance.

3. *Easier*. Marathons trashed my legs. Back then I'd try to "run out the lactic acid" the next morning, not yet realizing that this substance had little to do with my soreness. It was mainly muscle damage. Surprisingly I took less of a beating while going 70 miles. This left me with some blisters, sure, and sleep deprivation, certainly. But I ran the next day with little soreness.

I would never again to go anywhere near this far, let alone beyond. But this experience taught me what breaking up a run by stopping (and, later, walking) could make possible.

3. Foot Faults

(1974) IF EVER I needed walking as an additive or alternative to running, it was 1972-73. I'd raced too long and too often, rested too little, and had run myself into an injury that wasn't responding to any conventional or conservative medical treatment.

What my ailing foot craved the most, a break from running, I refused to give it. Finally there was no longer any choice about stopping. I feared this could be the Big One, the injury that stopped me permanently.

No running injury is minor if it happens to you. None is minor if interferes with your running. None is minor it won't go away. Mine seemed minor only at its start, a normal after-effect of running long.

One Saturday early in 1972, I took the two-hour run that was customary on non-race weekends. The next morning my left heel was sore. That's odd, I thought. This is my *good* heel, not the one that had been lumpy and tender to the touch since age 12.

Of course I didn't let this latest injury stand in the way of continued running. Long runs often left me sore-footed. I thought the pain would disappear, as always, in a few days. This problem stuck around.

At first I didn't have a name for it other than "bruise" and treated it as lightly as that. I raced 20 miles the next weekend, and 18 the week after that – and ran other long races periodically for two more months. The last of those was my final sub-three-hour marathon, at Avenue of the Giants in 1972.

By the time I visited the Munich Olympics that summer, an ugly lump had formed on the upper back of the heel bone. This spot the size of a thumb tip glowed red from the irritation and inflammation. My runs had shortened and slowed, and racing had disappeared. This was more than a bruise. But what, exactly, and what to do about it?

Finally I saw a general-practice doctor. "Bursitis," he called it. "Take a week off," he ordered. I did, and it didn't help. "Take two weeks off," this doctor told me at our follow-up appointment. Again, no improvement.

"It looks like you're going to need *months* off instead of weeks," he said. "And if that doesn't work, you might need to find another sport." Instead I found another doctor.

Dr. Steve Subotnick, a podiatrist, called me in late 1972 to ask if I'd be interested in hearing about his research on running injuries and their treatment. He wanted to write about it for *Runner's World* and invited me to visit his Saturday clinic for injured athletes.

I wanted to talk first about *my* injury, and he fit me in among a dozen other runners for an exam. He quickly diagnosed my problem as a "rectocalcaneal exostosis." A rectal what? "That's a bony growth on your heel bone," he explained. "The bigger it grows, the more it irritates the surrounding tissue. You need to make some changes that will ease the irritation."

Dr. Subotnick prescribed stretching exercise for my woeful state of inflexibility, recommended better shoes for my foot type, fashioned heel lifts and arch supports from strips of felt, and never said to stop running but to "run as pain allows." The pain continued, so he treated it with ultrasound. When that didn't work as quickly and thoroughly as we'd hoped, he shot me with cortisone.

21

Even then, the pain seriously limited my running. And even then, this podiatrist didn't recommend shopping for another sport. Instead he concluded that my injury had passed beyond the reach of conservative treatments. Only then did he mention surgery, which he said should *not* mean the end of running but could bring a new beginning.

SURGICAL SOLUTION

After months of denial and many more of trying treatments that didn't work well enough, I had little left to lose. I chose the last hope for relief.

"I'm ready for surgery," I told Dr. Steve Subotnick in early 1973. He agreed that "it's the way we need to go." When I asked how soon, he said, "How about next Tuesday?"

That was four days away, which didn't give my imagination much time to run wild. Then he had to postpone the operation for several more days, which gave time for dread to erode the hope: What if the knife slipped? What if the expected month off my feet stretched to several months, or forever?

This was to be relatively minor surgery, without general anaesthesia, as a short-stay patient who'd go home the same day. The doctor would go in and chisel away the excess bone at the heel, then sew me up. Almost as simple as pulling an infected tooth. But "minor surgery" is someone else's. If Dr. Subotnick took a chunk out of my heel bone, that was major enough for me.

The doctor said I could be confident of full recovery from this procedure – and that by hurting a lot for a little while I could avoid hurting a little for a long time. I placed my faith in his good judgment and firm hand. But even he couldn't control the slight chance that something would go wrong and that I'd be stuck for life with a defective foot.

A shot at waist level deadened both legs. A drape blocked me from seeing the gory details down below. Finally Dr. Subotnick told a student, "You can close it up now." Then a nurse held up a clear plastic pill bottle and said, "Here's the troublemaker." Floating in pink liquid were two rough-edged white chunks with stringy red thread attached. As recently as that morning these parts of me had sawed into soft tissue when I ran.

"Normally casts are optional in cases like this," said Dr. Subotnick. "I put some patients into a walking boot right away. But I know you runners. You're like hyperactive 12-year-olds. If I didn't give you a hard cast, you'd be out trying to run in two days and would mess up the good work we've done on you here."

He slapped on extra strips of plaster, "just to make sure you don't try anything funny," and ordered me onto crutches for the next week. "Then I'll add a heel so you can walk on the cast. You'll be out of it three weeks from now."

I wore through the walking cast twice before Dr. Subotnick freed me from this leg-prison. "How long until I can run again?" I asked him that day. He said, "Don't try until the stitches come out in another week."

I tried the running same day he unstitched me, four weeks after the surgery. I lasted one lap of a high school track, shuffled it in five minutes as walkers passed me. Never had so little meant so much.

The distance and pace picked up quickly from there. Another, different injury inevitably awaited in my not-too-distance future – along with a chance to recover by walking.

KEEPING GOING

My 1974 book *Run Gently, Run Long* reported that the foot surgery was successful, allowing me to run a marathon seven months later, then to set one last PR a few years after that. The bigger lesson, though, was that I hadn't fully appreciated the running – not big efforts of racing, but the simple act of running itself – until I'd almost lost it. I would seek ways to keep that from happening again, including some noted in this excerpt from the *Gently* book:

Few runners continue for decades, and the reasons for quitting are many. Some are disabled by chronic injuries. Some are discouraged by unfulfilled goals, but some also are satisfied by fulfilled ones and feel they have nothing left to prove.

If you are running to last, it might be best *not* to set high goals for yourself. The only goal should be to keep going. To do that, you have to stay healthy for running and happy with it. You have to find your joy in the everyday journey, not from some illusive destination.

The pursuit of excellence is so fast and hard that runners who choose this route often don't stay on it for long – "long" in this case meaning 10, 20 or more years, with no need or wish to stop. Pursuing excellence means suffering, sacrificing and gambling. It's tough to keep doing that unless you keep meeting your own high standards, and no one can succeed that way indefinitely.

Running long requires pacing. A miler can't start at sprinter's pace and expect to finish, and a marathoner can't go out like a miler. That's obvious. Pacing is also a weekly, monthly, yearly, *careerly* concept. This isn't so obvious, but is more crucial to long-run health and happiness.

Look at your running career as if it's a race, then pace yourself accordingly. One year is like the first mile of a marathon, so don't put the whole thing at risk by going out too fast. Instead, settle into a pace that you can continue all the way.

Runners who go hardest and fastest usually reap the greatest success, but their pace also kills them off early. Runners who go slower and easier aren't likely to win big, but their more casual pace keeps them going longer. They don't have to go very hard to outrun people who have dropped out.

This isn't to suggest that gentle pacers can't be fast sometimes, or can't have high-level success for awhile and still enjoy decades of running. It's just a warning against suffering, sacrificing and gambling *all* the time. The odds are stacked against those who try that.

The secret to long running life is summed up in six words from Larry Lewis, who died at 106 and had run for more than 90 of those years: "Keep moving and don't fight yourself."

Keep moving. Lewis said, "The minute I hear a man say he's going to lie in the sun and enjoy his retirement, I know he's about to meet his maker."

Don't fight yourself. It's a no-winner contest. If you look at yourself as an enemy to be beaten, who can you look to as a friend when you're hurting?

Runners who keep going are friendly with themselves, they grow and adapts to changing conditions as they go, and they find that their greatest pleasure is in where they are now, not in where they have been or where they might be headed. Runners who want to go long can heed Robert

Louis Stevenson, who wrote, "I travel not to go anywhere but to *go*." Look for ways to keep going.

4. Leg Savers

(1975) A LOVELY FEATURE of published writing is that you don't need to read and heed it right away. It's there, waiting, whenever you're ready for it.

Dr. Ernst van Aaken first told me, by way of an article he published in 1960, that I might profit by slowing down, going longer and walking more. I was a high school senior that year when *Track & Field News* offered a new publication – a technical quarterly filled with training advice. It was to be edited by my absentee coach, Fred Wilt, and he was to introduce me to a future mentor, Dr. van Aaken.

His opening lines in the first article in the first issue of *Track Technique* read, "According to my observations children are born long-distance runners. Any healthy boy or girl is able to run great distances at a moderate pace. The play of children is nothing more than a long-distance run, because in a couple of hours of play they cover many kilometers with several hundred pauses. The play of children is a primal form of interval training."

In 1960, I thought I'd outgrown my childish ways. My running was no longer playful as I followed the teachings of Hungarian-born coach Mihaly Igloi, running hard and fast intervals. His runners were the best in the U.S. at that time, and I tried to imitate them.

This training broke me down. I'd run slowly to recover, then would run myself into another breakdown, again and again – until finally in 1966 I decided to make all my running "recovery" running.

Dr. van Aaken was there again that year, reminding me in print what had happened: "The continual practicing of high speed, beyond racing speed, is uneconomical and leads to decreases in reserves." He recommended limiting high-speed running to five percent of total mileage.

By 1970, I'd embraced Ernst van Aaken as a guru and was writing about him. I quoted him selectively to support my LSD ideas but shut out what I wasn't yet ready to hear. For instance:

"The 'classical' interval training program is running long distances with rhythmical changes of pace. It is the method by which Emil Zatopek surprised the world of athletics in 1948 [by winning the Olympic 10,000; four years later, he swept the 5000, 10,000 and marathon gold medals].

"This method was fundamentally new in that Zatopek ran at sub-racing speed over distances that would have been thought impossible earlier – covering 30 to 50 kilometers [19 to 31 miles] almost every day. He told me his main training was 60 to 100 x 400 meters, each in 1:36 [about 6:30 mile pace, while his racing speed was almost two minutes faster]. He never stopped. He just interrupted the runs with 200 meters of very slow jogging.

"Then everyone misunderstood what Zatopek was doing. For instance, in Germany they said, 'Okay, we're going to run 200 meters very fast with very short pauses.' Everything went *kaput*. Performances went down. This type of interval training spread like a plague throughout the world."

Van Aaken talked in a 1974 *Runner's World* interview about the training of Harald Norpoth, his prize pupil and the 5000-meter silver medalist at the Tokyo Olympics:

"When he first came to train with my athletes, I had to

28

teach him to run slowly. By 'slowly' I mean 400 meters in two minutes [about 8:00 per mile]. He'd do it 10 times, 4000 meters total, as a start. This would be 350 meters of running, a minute of walking, then again slowly for 350 meters."

The interviewer, Tom Sturak, broke in: "But surely Norpoth did more than 10 times 400 meters!"

Of course, said van Aaken. "He followed that 'warmup' with 200 meters [1¼ miles] a minute slower than his best pace. Then he did 10 more slow 400-meter runs, then another 2000, and on and on until he ran 17 or 18 kilometers [about 11 miles] that way."

The doctor added that "even the little children in Waldniel [his German hometown] run that way," not as training but as active play. He told of following the activity of his own son:

"In two hours he covered a total of 10 kilometers – with 400 pauses. And after this he showed no fatigue. He could have gone on all day." The boy was six years old.

WALK DOC'S TALK

At first I'd merely skimmed Dr. Ernst van Aaken's 1960 article "Speed or Endurance Training?" which seemed to have little to do with me. His praise of walking certainly didn't. Not then, anyway, and not for a long time to come.

Fifteen years and many training changes later I still hadn't overcome my lingering resistance to taking walks during runs. Then a pair of events aligned perfectly during a single week in 1975. One was my first meeting with this German medical physician and coach, during his West Coast lecture tour. He delivered his talk in San Francisco from a wheelchair, the result of losing both legs after being struck down by a car while running three years earlier.

Van Aaken topics ranged widely in this lecture and our personal conversations, lasting eight hours in all. He breezed through the subject of run/walk intervals in five minutes, repeating what he'd been saying for years but I hadn't been ready to hear:

"Run as a child runs. Run playfully, for 10 kilometers a day, without pain or fatigue. The plan is the same for everyone from competing athletes to people recovering from heart attacks. Only the pace and the amount of walking varies."

Even his fastest runners trained this way, covering distances greater than 10K but seldom going far between walk breaks. By the time I finally met van Aaken, he had coached not only Olympic medalist Harald Norpoth, but also advised two world record-setters in the marathon, Liane Winter and Christa Vahlensieck.

I might have missed the walk-doc's point yet again if not for an episode that same week in 1975. A sore calf, injured in a race earlier that month, stopped me early in a Saturday group run. I waved the other runners on, then swore and kicked at the ground for having to quit the highlight run of my week.

Walking sullenly back toward the parking lot, I realized that the pain had eased. I ran again until the muscle threatened to spasm, walked until it loosened, ran a little farther than before, and ran/walked some more while letting the tender leg dictate the mix.

This slow-interval session continued for two hours that day – this after failing to run two miles steadily. The intervals were just what the doctor, Ernst van Aaken in this case, would have ordered. I've since learned that almost any injury responds better to intermittent than to uninterrupted running. Run/walk is, above whatever else it offers, a leg-saver.

Once healed from that calf injury, I tucked away the run/walk trick for future use. I would employ it often for injury first-aid, but walking wasn't yet ready to join my repertoire for *avoiding* injuries.

HIGH HIKE

High points in a runner's life take many forms: the fastest time, the longest distance, the races won, the records set. I'd already gone as high as I could in those ways that runners usually judge success. But I could still go higher – literally. The chance came when Don McMahill invited me in 1975 to his Camp Crockett in the Colorado Rockies.

While walking out of the Colorado Springs airport, Don motioned toward the highest point on the horizon and said off-handedly, "That's Pikes Peak. Runners will be climbing it on Sunday."

I hadn't planned to be among them, which was fine with him. "If you write anything about our camp," he said, "please don't give the impression that it's a Pikes Peak training center. Runners come to Crockett for lots of other reasons."

The camp brought together high school runners, college men, women, masters, fitness runners. But the camp remained intimately linked to the Pikes Peak race because of their proximity on the map and calendar. Some campers came specifically for this climb. Others ended up on the mountain in spite of themselves.

I came to camp only as a speaker but caught the "mountain fever" that was going around. My entry came too late for any training on the mountain or at this altitude. The ascent *started* almost as high as I had raced before, then went up almost 8000 more feet to peak at 14,115.

Joan Ullyot, a veteran of this course, oriented me by saying, "The trail near the top alternates between loose gravel and boulders. Almost everyone walks at this level, and 30-minute miles are not uncommon. Expect to take as long to do the half-marathon to the top as you'd normally need to finish a marathon."

Rick Trujillo, the king of this mountain, had won here the past two years and would again this time. He told the campers, "The secret for me is that I try to maintain my equilibrium at all times. I try to keep my breathing normal. If I get tired, I slow down.

"Near the top I may walk for 20 or 30 steps until I feel like running again. And I stop and drink every chance I get. I don't try to keep an even pace. On the mountain every step is different from every other."

I learned that my breathing wouldn't be normal here even if I laid down. Near the peak I ran 20 to 30 steps, if that, between long walks. The last mile took most of the half-hour that Joan Ullyot had promised, and the 13-mile climb took full marathon time plus a little more.

I walked because that was the only way I could get to the top. The lesson that I took down from this peak: you do what it takes to keep going. If walking is the best you can do to get where you want to go, that's good enough.

5. Osler's Teachings

(1980) I OWE Tom Osler more than I can ever repay by writing an introduction to his book and editing it for him. In a sense I owe two careers to him – one as a long-distance runner and the other as an author on running.

The best thing about working together on his second book was that I finally met Tom after knowing of him through his writing for more than a decade and borrowing plenty of those ideas. Now I was able to thank him.

Tom Osler was a seed-man. Back in 1966, I discovered his full-grown ideas at just the right time – as similar ones of my own were sprouting. He wrote a slim, roughly produced first book called *The Conditioning of Distance Runners*. It said some outrageous things for the time – such as that 90 percent of the running should be done at a comfortable pace. Remember, this was still the interval-training, pain-equals-gain era of running.

I was ready to accept what Tom was saying, because I'd had more than enough intervals and pain by then. I borrowed from him, and from Arthur Lydiard and Ernst van Aaken, adding my own modifications and claiming the mixture as something original in my own little book.

LSD came out a full three years after Tom's and added little to his concept except a cute name. It sold far more copies than his only because it was better produced and promoted. Other articles, booklets and books of mine followed, and they all traced their roots back to Tom Osler.

The running world took a while to catch up with Tom. But when it did, his ideas on combining gently paced base training with a period of carefully planned sharpening for races weren't at all outrageous anymore. They worked, and most runners now trained much like Osler – without knowing him as one source of what they did.

Tom's *Conditioning* booklet became a classic on training. But those who read it found that 32 pages didn't tell them enough. And by the late 1970s Osler himself knew he had more to say.

Fortunately for him and for us, he was talked into writing at length on what he had learned since 1966. The book that resulted gave Tom more credit for his early work and gave him a second chance to describe it. But more importantly, it was a new chance to say things that again might have sounded outrageous at the time but would become accepted ways of running within a few years.

He said, for instance, that stretching exercises may be dangerous. He said walking should be a regular part of running training. The ideal drink for long runs was heavily sugared tea. Ultramarathons could be completed by people without superhuman ability.

Tom said these things with the certainty of a scientist who had tested them before he wrote about them. He had the certainty of one who had run and raced since the Eisenhower presidency, who had won national championships when Johnson was in office, and who had run for 24 straight hours after Carter was elected.

Tom Osler had tried just about everything in running, and he knew what grew when the right seeds were planted.

UNSUNG GENIUS

Hundreds of running books have passed through the presses since I first read one in 1958. Too many of them moved me too much to name a single favorite, but I could give a short list.

Certain to make it would be the *Serious Runner's Handbook*, which didn't sell well enough in its day (published in 1978) and fell into out-of-print obscurity too soon. Its author, Tom Osler, is so little recognized now that I call him an "unsung genius." A genius because of what he wrote in the modern sport's formative years. Unsung because he never opted to become a star in print and on stage.

Thick-legged and slow as a young runner, his friends mocked him with the nickname "Turtle." He was forced to make up with cunning for what he lacked in runner body and speed. He was successful enough in this quest that he won several national long-distance championships.

Osler never was a running writer by trade. A friend, *Long Distance Log* publisher Browning Ross, had to talk him into penning Tom's slim booklet on training. *Conditioning of Distance Runners* laid the foundation for the *Serious* book. I helped talk him into writing that one.

Tom was a college math professor at Rowan University in New Jersey. He viewed running as a long series of problems to be solved, then described his solutions quickly and clearly. His *Handbook* covered 255 numbered topics in barely half that many pages, giving more good, practical information per paragraph than some writers do in a chapter.

He sprinkled the book with advice on the benefits walk breaks and how best to take them. An early hint of what would follow appeared in Lesson 1 that we're designed "to cover great distances with relatively little strain by walking, and perhaps walking and slow running."

Lesson 7 noted that he trained for ultras by "alternately running two miles, then walking a quarter-mile. Very few runners use this training technique today. This is unfortunate."

Lesson 31 told how long he walked and at what pace: "I find it convenient to walk briskly for five minutes. More walking seems to leave my legs heavy and unwilling to run again. Be sure to walk with vigor, as it is necessary to keep the circulation moving. Don't stroll as you would at a shopping mall."

Lesson 38 reported, "I can run up to 25 miles comfortably at a continuous pace. However, I like to mix walking with running so as not to be overly tired at the end." Later lessons told how well this technique had worked for him in a 24-hour race.

DOUBLING DISTANCE

Tom Osler's book didn't address the effects of walking less than five minutes at a time, or running shorter than 15 to 20 minutes. Later proponents of these breaks, notably Jeff Galloway, would have to provide their own answers.

After the book's publication, *Runner's World* asked Tom to write more about taking walks during a run. He stated in that 1979 article, "Runners can instantly double their longest nonstop distance by taking the walk breaks."

I took this to mean that anyone could go out today, with no special preparation, and far exceed normal limits. If you had recently run steadily for 10 kilometers, you could instantly complete a half-marathon with breaks. If a half-marathon was your longest without any stops, you could finish a marathon with them.

Osler didn't add, but could have, that the longer of the two wouldn't feel any harder. He did address the skeptics who argued, "I've had to walk in my runs, and I can hardly start again."

That's a different type of walking, he explained. It's walking because you *had* to, because exhaustion forced you to stop, and energy and enthusiasm were gone. His breaks weren't like that. You took them voluntarily, before you pooped out, as a means of stretching available resources.

If you didn't like the word "walk," said Osler, think of is another form of interval running. Pausing between fast segments is a perfectly honorable and acceptable speed-building practice. Intervals not only allow runners to go faster; they also help them go longer.

I already knew that from my 70 miles of run/*rest* (not walk), which had more than doubled my longest uninterrupted distance. But that experience was almost a decade old before I truly tried walk breaks in a race. After editing Tom Osler's advice, I thought: Worth a try someday. That day wasn't long in coming.

FIRST WALKS

Walking wasn't in the plan for my next marathon after coming under Tom Osler's influence. At Boston 1979, I ran the usual way, crashed in the late miles and walked most of the final one at double the pace of the previous 25.

A photo taken then shows a look of shame, as if revealing my failure. My next photo from a marathon, Summit 1980, shows me finishing strongly. A closer shot would have revealed a smile of success.

The difference between those two races? Walk breaks, employed at the second one for the first time in a marathon.

Circumstances conspired to put me at the latter starting line woefully undertrained. An achilles-tendon injury had struck in fall 1980, limiting me to no run longer than one hour for two months before the Summit Marathon. I'd never gone into a race this long with training runs so short.

Summit wasn't a "flat and fast" marathon. As the name suggests, this race had a single hill – a climb of 2000 feet to the rim of the San Francisco Bay Area's Coast Range in the first half, then down again to a sea-level finish.

There never was a better place or time to test walk breaks. I intended to follow tan Osler-like plan: run 25 minutes, then walk five. Maybe finishing a marathon wouldn't be possible, but doubling my longest recent distance would still be a good day's work.

Two problems arose early: Stopping while others kept running proved embarrassing, and a five-minute walk seemed interminably long. New plan, devised on the fly: run the two miles or three between drink stations (where many runners stopped with me), and walk for two or three minutes (while pretending to drink slowly). This was an early glimpse at a mix that would later become standard for me: walking about one minute per mile.

This run/walk pattern had payoffs immediate and long-term. It let me get through that marathon without undue struggle. I climbed and descended the Coast Range in good shape, thanks to the breaks. I set a PW – personal worst of 3:36 – but the walks has slowed my pace much less than expected. This time was only eight minutes slower than my run-only PW.

This first run/walk experience also previewed my future practice and advice. I would never again try to *run* a marathon. And I would recommend that marathoners take shorter run and walk intervals than those Osler prescribed.

6. Theories Practiced

(1989) MY 1980S started with a walk-break marathon. The decade ended the same way. In between, though, I hardly walked at all. Didn't reject it, just didn't need it.

Life became chaotic for me in the eighties. I left *Runner's World*, lost the replacement job at *Running* magazine (when it folded) and returned to *RW*. I moved from California to Oregon, then turned down an offer to relocate in Pennsylvania (where *RW* had moved).

One of my children, Eric, was diagnosed as deaf. Daughter Leslie was born multiply handicapped. My marriage ended early in the decade, and I didn't meet my next wife-to-be until the late 1980s.

Scrambling to support two households, I wrote too many books that didn't sell well. I traveled too much, as a paid speaker, trying to fill the income gap.

With time tight and energy low, my running didn't amount to much. For most of the eighties I rarely raced and never ran longer than an hour at a time. I never uttered the R-word, retired, but with each new year it looked like the 1980 Summit Marathon would stand as my last.

Walking became a theoretical exercise. I wrote articles in praise of this practice (including one beneath the next subtitle here) and spoke highly of it in talks to running groups (influencing few readers or listeners to try this at home). Yet I did very little of it myself anymore.

39

BEYOND THE BOOM

Running fell to a low ebb by the mid-1980s, well down in numbers of participants and events from when newbies had flooded into the sport a decade earlier. Post-running boom pessimism prompted me to write the following for *Runner's World* in April 1986:

Life's little irritants include the pronouncements of trend-spotters who assume, or hope, that running is a fad in the last throes of its natural life cycle. It first was the secret of the few, then was "discovered" by the media and promptly oversold to panacea-seekers, and finally was "exposed" as boring at best and dangerous at worst. Disillusioned and disabled ex-runners are now said to be choosing more exciting and safer activities.

So begins a new cycle. Just as the sins of sedentary existence were once used to convert runners, promoters of alternative activities now play up the negative side of running to justify replacing it with the Next Big Thing.

Aerobic dance set to music is "more fun." Fitness gained from weight machines is "total." Swimming is cooler (in both senses of the word), bicycling covers more distance faster, and both sports free the legs from ground-pounding.

No argument here. I won't compare the strong and weak points of exercises – except to say that most of those claiming to be "better" than running are also more exotic and expensive. They often require instructors, equipment or access to special facilities beyond what a runner needs.

One notable exception this more-flash/more-cash rule: walking. The simple, humble old walk is enjoying new attention as a fitness choice.

Promoters and trend-spotters alike are touting walking as a safe haven for retired runners. Running and walking are pictured as competing exercises, as either/or choices.

In fact, they more closely resemble relatives than rivals. Walking offers us confirmed runners more promise as a complement to running than as a replacement for it.

We're the people who refuse to believe, or even to care, that running was a "fad." By refusing to fade away, we irritate the trend-spotters who wait to pronounce this fad dead. We never want to stop running, but we're always looking for ways to run better.

In steps walking. I'm here now to praise the walk, not condemn it – and maybe to change your mind if you still share my old negative feelings.

We're talking here about a special kind of walking: brief walks blended into a primarily running program with specific purposes in mind. These aren't long-distance hikes, not race walks, not aimless strolls– all fine activities in their own place, but this isn't it.

I propose, and practice, walking selectively to make the long runs longer, the fast runs faster and the easy runs easier. You've heard my "longer" stories: how I once PRed in distance at 70 miles (in a 100-mile race, alas) by stopping to rest every few miles, and how I finished a marathon with walk breaks after training no longer than one-quarter that distance in recent months (due to an injury).

As for speed, did I tell you about my 2:28 marathon? That would have been a PR by more than 20 minutes – except that my actual time was 24 hours. This was an all-day relay, one mile at a time with nearly an hour's rest between as teammates ran. My miles averaged 5:38, a minute per mile faster than I could have raced a marathon nonstop.

Okay, this is an extreme example of recovery breaks. I didn't walk much between intervals, but mainly sat or laid down to wait for the next round. Yet this experience alerted me to the potential of recovery breaks for extending speed limits at more normal lengths.

Lately I haven't raced much and have missed the feeling of pushing the pace that way. So I've simulated 5K racing, not with a full-bore time trial but with a set of intervals adding up to 3.1 miles. Thanks to the brief walk breaks, total running time has been faster than what I could have raced.

Recently walking has also given me back my mornings. I'd long been an early runner, until my feet and legs betrayed me. They rebelled against going directly from the bed to the road, so my running moved later and later into the day.

Then I tried walking first thing each morning before starting to run. A 10- to 20-minute walk worked better at easing stiffness and soreness than delaying the start for hours.

STARTING OVER

Every marathon, no matter how many times you've gone this far before, begins with a question: "Can I finish this (again)?" More than ever, this was my worry on the latest marathon morning, as I broke a nine-year absence from this event at Long Beach, California, in 1989. I was in no shape before the start for a coherent conversation, let alone one being recorded for national television.

42

"Let's try again," said interviewer Marty Liquori. "That sounded okay, but you didn't answer my question about why you picked Long Beach?" He was taping the opening segment for ESPN's "Running and Racing" report. We stood in front of the starting line with the final countdown underway, and I'd just blown the first take. My second try was barely better, and we didn't have time for a third.

My shakiness in the interview didn't come from standing before a camera, which I'd done often the past few years. The tension came from facing a marathon for the first time since 1980. My running hadn't stopped in the meantime, of course, but I had never raced beyond 13.1 miles, and even then only on impulse and memory rather than with specific training.

You can do that at the shorter distances. You can wake up on race day, decide it's the right day for a 5K or 10K, and get along because you run about that far every day. But you can't fake a marathon. You can't finish one without planning and training.

Liquori's first question had begun with "Why...?" So I launched into a garbled explanation about starting over in the marathon. I tried to say that marathoners had changed since my first written words of advice came out in the 1970s, and so had I.

At that time most of us were experienced runners, trying to qualify for Boston or to earn a line in *Runner's World*, which then listed all sub-three-hour men and sub-four women each year. A shrinking percentage of marathoner could do that now, so most of them ran (or ran/walked, by choice or necessity) mainly to finish. I'd become one of them.

Because marathoners had changed, so had my advice to them. It was more conservative now. I recommended the least training that we could get by with rather than the most we could do. It was time for me to see if this plan really worked. For me.

But that's not what Liquori had wanted to know. "What I asked," he said, "was why did you choose the Long Beach Marathon?" I told him that at about 4000 runners it was the right size, big enough to provide company all the way but never crowded. I added that giving a talk here the year before, then watching the race, had triggered the thought of trying another marathon.

Then in December 1988, on a whim, I entered and completed a half-marathon in Las Vegas. Later I thought: If I can do this with no special training, maybe a little bit more training will take me twice as far. Soon after that, Long Beach director Joe Carlson invited me to his marathon – not to write about it or to speak at it this time, but as an entrant.

So for the first time in almost nine years I planned to try a marathon. Over the next four months I went long every other week, each longer than the last. This was my first time to train with run/walk on the long days.

The extended training period was part of my ongoing fascination, now revived, with the marathon. The uncertainty of race day is another strange attraction. No matter how well you've prepared, you can't assume that a marathon will end well until it's over. That's why I woke up on marathon morning worrying…

Would the knee and calf pains that had surfaced in the long run/walks worsen on this even longer one? Had too much time passed between my last long run and the marathon (five weeks, as a cold made me abandon the longest scheduled session)? And had my longest in training been long enough?

Each worry vanished. The planning and training worked as well as I could have hoped. I met my one true goal: to finish. This yielded my slowest marathon time so far, 3:48, but I also had one of my easier times getting there.

My question about going this distance, after avoiding it for so long, finally had another answer. Even out beyond the length of my longest pre-marathon run/walk (three hours, running five minutes and then walking one), and even in the unusual warmth (high temperature about 70 and humid after training in rainy coolness), I didn't really crash.

The walking totaled 28 minutes, or only slightly more than the scheduled one minute per mile. Through 20 miles the walks lasted two or three minutes at each drink station. At mileposts 20 to 23, I walked a minute each time. From then on in I reverted to the training plan of run five minutes, walk one.

The pace, including walks, averaged 8:46 overall. Excluding the walks, I ran about eight-minute miles. That's faster than I'd gone in a non-stop *half*-marathon last December. The walks worked.

7. Best Tests

(1995) MY RE-ENTRY into the marathon was brief. After the 1989 Long Beach race, three more years passed before tackling it again. I wasn't physically unable, just busy remarrying and forming a new household with Barbara and two of my children.

By 1992 daughter Sarah had started college. Son Eric was attending a residential school for the deaf. I wanted to run another marathon, and my wife wanted to travel. We combined our interests by stretching the race weekend into a mini-vacation at a pleasant place: Avenue of the Giants in the northern California redwoods.

We enjoyed that trip so much that marathon travel became a twice-a-year habit through 1995. We went from the Pacific (Honolulu) to the Atlantic (New York City) and into Canada (Victoria). The flurry of eight marathons in four years was my largest total in a similar time span since the early 1970s.

This series of marathons also provided my best sustained testing of how walking worked under various weather and course conditions, as well as with variable (and usually minimal) training. I hadn't yet settled into a standard run/walk routine but was trending toward shorter run segments than before *and* shorter walk breaks.

Records from this marathon series were even more detailed than usual. I checked and recorded the total amount of walking, along with the usual stats on training and racing times. Then as now I trained by time without calculating the distance covered.

These are the results (+ = fastest time, most walking, longest training; - = slowest time, least walking, shortest training):

Marathon completed	Final time	Total walk	Long run
Ave. of Giants 1992	4:14	65 min.	3:00+
Honolulu 1992	5:01-	76 min.+	2:00-
Drake Relays 1993	3:56+	22 min.	2:17
Portland 1993	3:59	19 min.	2:07
Big Sur 1994	4:15	25 min.	2:00-
New York City 1994	4:14	21 min.	2:00-
Napa Valley 1995	4:00	17min.-	2:08
Royal Victoria 1995	4:02	27 min.	2:00-
Averages	*4:12*	*34 min.*	*2:11*

The first two races, those with the most walking (and resulting in a pair of PW times), were unusually hot – surprisingly so at normally cool Avenue of the Giants, and expectedly in ever-humid Honolulu. Also, an auto accident had banged me up a few days before the Hawaii trip.

In the last six of these marathons I averaged about a one-minute walk for every mile run. Typically I'd walk less often through 20 miles, then need more or longer walks (or both) at the end.

These results pointed to another benefit of walk breaks: I could get by on less training than when I'd tried to run all the way. My longest run/walk before the marathons (2:11) averaged little more than half my average finish time (4:12). Only once in all those years did I train as long as three hours.

Compare this to training for my eight *fastest* marathons. The last of them came almost a decade before I adopted run/walk. Their average time was 2:56. The longest time spent training for them averaged nearly 40 minutes *more* than race time – or about marathon length at a slower pace. (Many of these "training" runs actually were slow marathons or ultras.)

ENERGY SOLUTIONS

You might think the need for extra late-race walking was minimal-training related. I might have thought so too if not for an experiment, late in this 1992-95 series, with eating during marathons.

My habit had long been to run on empty. I subscribed to the Arthur Lydiard view of nutrition. The coach from New Zealand famously said, "I've never seen anyone collapse from malnutrition in a run. But I frequently see people run into trouble for the opposite reason: eating too much of the wrong things too close to race time. Better to leave well enough alone and not eat anything that morning."

I'd always taken my last food the night before, then nothing else caloric until afterward. The closest I came to a learning experience otherwise was at the 1979 Boston Marathon. Boston started later then than now, at high noon. This meant my "fast" lasted through midafternoon.

To break three hours that year, I needing just 10 minutes to travel the final 1.2 miles. In the time it took to think this thought, I was walking, and not by choice. This short distance stretched 18 long minutes, yielding a time of 3:08.

At the finish line a friend handed me a Coke. I chugged

it down, and it was like taking a quick-acting drug. Within minutes I ran back to my hotel, about a mile away. Oh, to have had that liquid sugar/caffeine a few miles sooner!

This lesson was lost on me then. Fully 15 years later I took advice from Jeff Galloway, for the first of many times to come. Told of my last-marathon slowdowns, he said, "Have you tried eating a PowerBar during the race?"

I hadn't, of course. The Olympian-turned-marathon mentor said during his annual running camp, "You're taking an extra hour or more to finish than you once did. You need more fuel. Try cutting a PowerBar into small pieces, and eat one each time you stop for a drink."

I adopted Jeff's plan at my next marathon, New York City 1994. Result: my first-ever negative split, the second half passing five minutes faster (or less slow) than the first. Thinking this might have been good luck unrelated to the portable food item, I retested the PowerBar plan at Napa Valley the next spring. This time the final half took 10 minutes less time than the opener.

If Tom Osler had heard this, and if he were an I-told-you-so kind of guy, he would have said, "What took you so long?" He had written about midrace fueling 15 years earlier.

In Chapter 4 here, I quoted his article about walk breaks. But in the timeline of this book I was only ready to practice half of his advice then. He had another tip for stretching available resources over longer distance.

That was to use sugared, caffeinated drinks. Osler's preference during his ultras was heavily sweetened tea. For reasons of health he shied away from both sugar and caffeine most of the time, and speculated that their energy boost was bigger because he hadn't developed a tolerance for these substances.

49

I too was breaking away from sugar and caffeine by the mid-1990s, to ease a chronic medical condition. Marathons had become my "ultras." My energy drink of choice, taken only in races and the longest training, was Snapple iced tea, peach flavored, naturally sweetened. Drink time came, as Tom Osler had said it should, during some of the walk times.

UNREAL?

Dissenters to my increasingly frequent walk-break references were, I'm sure, more numerous than they let on in the 1990s. Most of them kept their eye-rolling, not-this-again reactions to themselves or among close friends. Written complaints were rare, and those spoken to me were almost unheard of. Runners are generally too polite or care too little to comment. An exception rated this report in my 1995 book *Better Runs*:

The logo on his T-shirt should have warned me even if the look on his face hadn't done so. The face wore frown lines of disagreement as he put up his hand after my talk. The shirt read "Western States 100."

I missed both signals while motioning for him to have his say. We'd come to my favorite part of these programs, the question/comments portion when I get to talk *with* runners and not just at them.

These clinics aren't "Meet the Press." The questioning isn't usually a cross-examination, and the comments are seldom confrontational.

So I expected no strong dissent after finishing my spiel about trends in marathon training... about the near-perfect record of finishes by graduates of various organized training programs... about training mileage shrinking... about walking some if that's what it takes to finish... about median marathon times now being an hour slower than they were a decade earlier.

These points – all of which were facts, not opinions – stirred up the man in the Western States shirt. He said, "My question is, When is a marathon not a *real* marathon?" He then gave his own answer.

"In my book it doesn't really count if you plan to walk and you take all day to finish. I think there should be a stiffer qualification for counting as a real marathon than the one you allow. You might as well count people who use bikes, or roller-skate, or hitch rides in cars."

His scowl and the vehemence of his argument left me fumbling for a suitable reply. With the luxury of editing it now reads: In my book if you finish a marathon under your own power, it counts.

You see, the marathon isn't like any shorter race. The 10K is a race in which the question for most runners isn't, "Can I go the distance" but, "How fast?"

For most marathon entrants, on the other hand, this is a survival test. They survive the distance any way they can and take as long a time as needed, sort of exceeding the race's cutoff limit.

Races have every right to set reasonable time limits. Timing used to end at 4:00 at many marathons (or even 3:30 at my first Boston) because the bulk of the field was done by then. Now most races have more finishers above that time than below.

Grandma's Marathon, for instance, once ended officially at 4:00. The deadline is now two hours slower, which averages a generous 13:45 per mile. A soft pace but no stroll in the park.

51

I advised Ultraman to embrace the people who take hours longer than he does to finish. They are the future of marathoning at a time when the number of runners like him has slipped too low to sustain quality events.

In this country, size and success are synonymous. Successful events attract sponsor dollars and media interest, which in turn draws even more runners (and, yes, run/walkers).

Ultraman said he planned to run all the marathons that *Runner's World* named as the year's top 20 in this country. He would be vastly outnumbered there by the marathoners he'd call less than "real." Their going the distance in their way makes it possible for him to run in his.

8. New Marathoners

(1996) A REVOLUTION of sorts was taking shape in the early 1990s. It was the first rumblings of what came to be known as the "second running boom."

The first, starting 20 years earlier, featured mostly young males (like myself at the time). Simply running long wasn't good enough; it had to be long, fast. Qualifying for Boston was the driving ambition of marathoners. Hardly anyone took as long as five hours to finish, and not many topped four.

Running then passed through a quiet time in the 1980s. The speedsters aged, often beating themselves into early retirement, and they weren't replaced in significant numbers by the new young. Race size shrunk, and races disappeared. The number of marathons fell by half during the eighties.

This wasn't the end of running but merely a pause before a new beginning. This came in the 1990s, which brought a new boom. It was different from the first and would be bigger, if only because it was more inclusive. It featured more women, more older and slower runners (including many like me who'd been young and fast during the first boom), more emphasis on going the distance instead of racing, and more people willing to walk.

I caught my first glimpse of what the marathon was becoming while run/walking Avenue of the Giants in 1992. Here's what I wrote at the time, in a column titled…

53

MARATHON MILLIE

Their purple T-shirts with spotted-owl artwork identified who they were and what they'd just done. Ten of them had completed the Avenue Marathon, and now they were refueling and rehashing at a restaurant in Myers Flat, California. They didn't know me as I sat at another table, but my purple "finisher" shirt told them all they needed to know.

A woman of about 60 came over and introduced herself as Millie. "We're all from Portland," she said. "We like to travel to scenic marathons together – Crater Lake, Victoria and now Avenue." She asked if I knew any future possibilities for them.

Here they'd just finished one marathon and were already planning their next. The time-honored Frank Shorter Rule – that you can't think of running another marathon until you forget how bad the last one felt – didn't cover them.

They felt fine because they hadn't hurried. They were here to *have* a good time, not to run one. Their marathon wasn't a race but a long, slow run/hike. They'd be ready to take on another one like it in a few weeks.

If you haven't run this distance for awhile (as I hadn't in three years), or haven't drifted back through the ranks (as I had), you may not have noticed how much marathoning has changed. It isn't the sport it used to be.

It's really two sports now. One side still races for fast times and high places, while the other runs and walks to finish. The first sport is shrinking, the second growing.

Thirty percent of Boston Marathon runners broke 3:00 in 1972. Twenty years later, with a field eight times larger, the sub-three count has dropped to 10 percent.

The biggest marathon of spring 1992 was Los Angeles, where entries were unlimited. Only two percent of its nearly 20,000 finishers broke three hours.

Millie and friends represent the growth area of today's marathons. Their event is a graduation exercise from an organized training program (this group met at the Portland Marathon Clinic), a guided group tour, a social event, a mini-vacation.

The growth prospects of marathoning clearly lie with the "Millies." The most successful events of the future will be those catering to the needs and interests of these new marathoners – and to recovering racers (like me) who waltz over to the other side.

They don't need to train as hard as the racer. Their long runs can be shorter and less frequent, and they recover quicker. Some of these marathoners don't train long at all, but simply run a marathon every month or so.

The new marathoners are less interested in a flat-fast course than in the sights along the way. They're likely to choose Avenue of the Giants or Big Sur over a better-known marathon in a blander setting.

It's okay now to finish slowly. It's okay to take walk breaks or even to walk all the way. It's not okay to say that U.S. marathoning is poorer today because the front ranks have thinned. Our wealth has simply dropped back an hour or more to all the "Millies" of the sport.

DON'T KNOCK THE WALK

My increasingly frequent writings about walking led to criticism from an unexpected source in 1994. A column that year in my *Running Commentary* newsletter delved into perceived differences with a runner-turned-walker:

A certain group of running purists considers me something of a traitor to the cause for daring to suggest that we do anything but run. So I take care to say that mixing walking breaks into long runs isn't for everyone.

The idea slipped into the middle of a recent *Runner's World* column. I qualified this advice by saying only walk a little bit, only in the longest runs and only then if they're hard to finish any other way.

That column (cited in Chapter 7 here) addressed the question: Does the walking makes a marathon less than an honest effort? My answer: For most runners the marathon is a survival test that they get through any way they can and in as long as it takes.

I added: Marathoners should be trained well enough to run most of the distance. And race officials have the right to set time limits for finishers (of, say, six to seven hours).

I expected letters from pure runners, chastising me for daring to use the word "walk" at all. I didn't count on the strongest disagreement coming from a walker.

Bill Weldon wrote from San Jose, California. He has run marathons, run/walked them and is evolving now into purely a walker.

"I have always been a much better power-walker than runner," said Weldon. "I have walked 5K's and 10K's at a 12-minute pace, and I have been training to walk a marathon at 12½-minute pace, or 5½ hours. At the longer distances my run/walk and walk-only times end up about the same."

He then expressed "total disagreement with you when you say a person should be able to run most of the way. If a person can walk fast enough, what's the difference?"

Weldon added, "I've read all your books and columns, dating back to the mid-1970s." He suggested that I've strayed from my earlier course. By taking the time-limit stand, "you've abandoned the back-of-the-packer you once championed. Whatever happened to your philosophy of long, slow runs?"

LSD is alive and well, I told him. The walk breaks let me run longer than I could go without them. They also leave me a little slower. How could I abandon the back-of-the-packers when I'm growing closer to them all the time?

WALKING TALL

I played no role in three testimonials that reached me soon after publication of the essay above. This piece hadn't moved any of them to write to me, if they'd read it at all. All three run/walkers had reached their own conclusions apart from anything I might have written, which showed how widely this practice had spread by the mid-1990s.

The three letters arrived from a varied group – a young ultraman, a marathoner in his late 60s and a short-distance runner in his 50s. They walked in different ways – as respites in extra-long races, as regular breaks during most runs and as true race-walk training.

An article in *Ultrarunning* magazine told how Kevin Setnes won the national 24-hour run title while boosting his PR distance from 125 miles to 160. He alternated 25-minute runs with five-minute walks (which was how author

Tom Osler had introduced readers to run/walk in the late 1970s). He figured this pattern let him run at normal pace instead of a minute per mile slower than he was used to running.

Ultrarunning noted that Setnes's 25/5 formula had the support of eminent researchers Tim Noakes and David Costill. Dr. Noakes noted in *The Lore of Running* that runners use aerobic energy most efficiently for periods of 10 to 30 minutes. Dr. Costill wrote in *Inside Running* that walk breaks need to last at least four minutes to give the desired recovery.

Dr. Alex Ratelle would disagree with Costill's specific number, though not with walk breaks themselves. Ratelle was a 2:30 marathoner in his 50s, now running about an hour slower at 69.

The *Minneapolis Star Tribune* reported that Ratelle inserted six to eight short walks, less than a minute each, into his half-marathon training, and even a few of these breaks into shorter runs. This had been his practice for 20 years.

"I walk anywhere from 20 seconds to a minute," he said in the newspaper article. "You unload lactic acid and carbon dioxide during the walks. You give your liver a chance to get rid of the lactate, which is why your muscles are uncomfortable."

James McFadden contributed another variation on this theme. He competed as both a runner and race-walker in Oklahoma and surrounding states. At age 55 he ran a 5K in 18 minutes and walked it in 25.

"In almost 40 years in the sport," he said, "I've never had a serious injury. One reason is walking. I sometimes race-walk during running training, and I do days of race-walking between days of running training.

"I don't feel walking makes one less of a runner or a slower runner. Race-walking is my cross-training and my flexibility training."

McFadden's approach confounded his fellow runners. He recalled training on the same track as two rivals, they running 400-meter intervals while he walked his. A week later he met the same two men in a 5K road run, beating them both.

"How did you do that?" one asked McFadden. "We just saw you walking in training."

He smiled and said, "You guys have just got to stop training so hard." Then he added more seriously, "Actually walking is very hard training if you walk fast. But it is less stressful on your feet and legs than running. I never lose any running fitness in the weeks I take off to work on race-walk events."

9. Galloway's Way

(1998) IN THE MID-1990s walk breaks for marathoners gained a needed spokesman. Ernst van Aaken spoke and wrote only in German, and his messages hadn't translated well or traveled widely in English. Tom Osler worked as a math professor, not a walking promoter. I'd occasionally touted this practice in my writing but had wooed few converts.

In stepped Jeff Galloway. He brought impeccable credentials as a runner, a 1972 Olympian in the 10,000 and one of the better marathoners of his time – which happened to be the best era ever for American men.

Later Jeff founded running stores called Phidippides and organized summer running camps in scenic locales. He spoke often and well to running audiences. He wrote articles for running magazines and books for runners.

Meanwhile he experimented with walk breaks, to the point where he took them public in the 1990s with his Runwalkrun program. Training groups sprung up nationwide. Eventually more than 100,000 run/walkers would enjoy successful finishes, Jeff's way.

No individual was more responsible for the sport's second boom, at least for marathoners, than Jeff Galloway. He didn't invent walk breaks, but he did more than anyone else to popularize them.

As such, Jeff also became the chief lightning rod for critics who didn't equate popularity with legitimacy. As the number of run/walkers grew, so did the volume of criticism. The following piece, written in 1997, describes that verbal battling.

WALK WARS

Way back when, we fought holy wars over running pace. On one side of this battle line stood the old guard that believed it wasn't really training if it wasn't fast enough to hurt. Lining up on the other side were the rebels who practiced and promoted LSD-style running.

The traditionalists shouted that the LSDers were undercutting serious running, blaming them for a decline in U.S. racing performances. The LSDers countered that the speed killed the legs and spirit of its practitioners.

These two groups finally agreed to coexist in relative peace. Anyway, nearly everyone came to practice some slow running, even runners who won't stoop to calling it "LSD."

But while a truce has come to this front, a new holy war has broken out. It too has to do with pace and effort, now pitting run-every-step runners against the run-with-walk-breaks crowd.

I mentioned to a marathon race director that the numbers of entrants is growing again nationwide. "But do they run the distance," he asked, "or do they take those walking breaks?"

The trend away from marathon-as-race and toward marathon-as-survival-test bothered him. "Maybe we should give these people certificates of underachievement," he said. "I'm from the old school that believes the marathon is a *running* event."

He's far from alone. I've heard many such thoughts, usually privately expressed as this race director's were for fear of hurting his own entry numbers, that the walkers somehow cheapen the sport and don't really belong in the company of pure runners.

Reports reached me about the coach of a marathon training group who targeted Jeff Galloway for attack. The critic called Galloway's walking breaks "an unproven method" and a "marketing ploy." He told his runners that a marathon finish "doesn't count if you don't run all the way."

Come now, this isn't religion or politics. To walk or not to walk isn't a serious enough matter to draw verbal blood.

Walk breaks bring the marathon within reach of thousands more entrants. The breakers contribute heavily to the current robust health of the event, which is now the biggest – and slowest – in its history. They make the pure runners look faster, without having to work any harder.

If you believe that a marathon is only a run, then don't walk. But don't deny these breaks to the marathoners who can't or won't go this far without them.

JEFF'S JUDGES

Shortly after the "Walk Wars" column appeared, the fire directed at Jeff Galloway grew more personal and more public. He was up to the challenge, for reasons the following piece gave:

He showed up seven hours before the day's race start in Edmonton, Alberta. His fans and followers wouldn't arrive until later, and for now he was helping pitch a tent and set up tables and chairs for the day, though this wasn't his job here.

Jeff Galloway would answer questions and hand out advice and encouragement for hours. No question would be too small or repetitive for an answer, and no runner would be too humble for a tip and a good wish.

Watching Jeff in action, you couldn't imagine a less likely candidate for controversy. You'd never meet a more-interested-in-runners, more-dedicated-to-running guy.

He is one of the wise elders of the sport. But a certain group of critics can't forgive his success in attracting a following... or for not living in his Olympian past by advising only would-be Olympians... or for saying it's okay to be slow and – gasp! – even to walk.

The critics usually haven't gotten to know Jeff, haven't read him and haven't heard him speak. I've done all three, which is why the attacks annoy me so. He is almost a second brother to me, plus I feel another type of kinship with him.

In the 1970s I felt some of the wrath that he's feeling now. My booklet *LSD* (short for long slow distance) dared to recommend slower, easier training. I never claimed this was the one best way for everyone to run, only an option for some (like me) who'd fallen into speed traps.

Critics who didn't know me and never read the booklet cried "heresy." Some still say that LSD was a plague from which the sport hasn't fully recovered.

Jeff now faces much the same criticism, but more so. With a running populace 1000 times larger than I dealt with, there are that many more potential critics. Some of their comments are more harsh than any I ever heard.

Honest disagreement is expected and encouraged. But when it turns too personal, it must be exposed and answered.

Speaking out in the magazine *FootNotes* was Robert Johnson. He devoted six of his first 12 paragraphs to Jeff Galloway, and this wasn't an expression of devotion.

Johnson's column began mildly, with differences of opinion over approaches to running. Fair enough. But then Johnson shifted to "shredding" (his term) Galloway.

"It's disgraceful," he wrote, "that a former U.S. Olympic distance runner is dumbing down the sport we all love. Where's the admiration and respect for the elite competitive athletes who train their butts off?"

I've appeared with Jeff at races and camps dozens of times. He's consistently admiring and respectful of hard-training competitors. (His own two sons are outstanding athletes.) He simply chooses to spend most of his time advising never-to-be-elites.

Wrapping up his Galloway critique, Robert Johnson turned sarcastic: "I hope the tens of thousands of Galloway disciples don't have heart attacks if they learn that Jeff actually *ran* the entire 1972 U.S. Olympic Trials 10K."

Jeff is perfectly capable of answering the critics himself. But he rarely responds, even to the most wrong-headed and mean-spirited attacks.

Nor does he ask his many friends and followers to defend him. We do it anyway because we believe in him even more than in his methods.

GALLOWAY'S GALLANTRY

If you need still more evidence of what kind of person Jeff Galloway is, consider this story. It came from the peak year of his racing career and has nothing to do with walk breaks – but everything to do with why he became a such a great friend of the sport. He was a helper in 1972, and has remained so.

When you hear today that Jeff was an Olympian, you might assume that it was as a marathoner. He built much of his reputation as a coach, author and speaker around giving marathon advice, yet this wasn't the distance that took him to the Munich Games.

I happened to be at the 1972 Olympic Trials in Eugene, Oregon. The 10,000 started the meet, and the marathon ended it little more than a week later.

The latter was Jeff's better event, but he was a contender on the track as well. The same was true of his Florida Track Club teammate Frank Shorter, while another fellow FTC runner Jack Bacheler was stronger in the 10,000.

I'd met Jeff in Eugene the year before when my future hometown hosted the national marathon championship. By chance we had even shared a breakfast the morning after that race. Now I would cheer for him in his two Trials races.

Shorter won the 10, Galloway finished second, but Bacheler was nosed out for third. My best instant guess was that Jeff would later make the marathon team, then offer his track spot to Jack.

But wait. Bacheler was disqualified from the 10 for a bumping incident (a no-harm foul that didn't affect the finish order). Now he had to qualify in the marathon, his weaker event (mainly from relative lack of experience, not talent).

Jeff could have challenged Frank Shorter and Kenny Moore for the Trials title. Instead he stuck with Bacheler at an agreed-upon pace that was more cautious.

Shorter and Moore intentionally tied for first. The all-important third spot appeared that it might end in another tie as Galloway and Bacheler ran their final lap of the track together.

Then Jeff backed off a step, yielding the qualifying place to his Florida teammate. They would have preferred to switch events at the Olympics, but officials wouldn't hear of it.

So while Jeff didn't qualify for the final in Munich, the U.S. marathoners posted their best finish ever at the Games. Shorter in first, Moore in fourth and Bacheler in ninth would have won the team title if there had been such an award.

Jeff must have wondered what might have been if allowed to run that marathon. Yet, after he became one of my best friends in the sport, I never heard him voice any regrets over his choice to help a friend. This helps explain why Jeff became the revered figure he is.

10. Time Out

(1998) MY MAGAZINE and newsletter columns were lectures-on-paper. After I'd had my say, readers got theirs. Whether they agreed or disagreed, corrected or amplified, I enjoyed switching from talking at them to hearing from them.

Cathy Troisi of Seneca Falls, New York, became a regular pen-pal after she'd first written to chide me for comments made in a mid-1990s *Runner's World* column. I'd written there that "the marathon is, after all, a running event." The walking breaks I recommended – and used – accounted for small fraction of total time and were meant only to extend the running range.

Cathy disagreed with my definition of the marathon as a "run," saying she thought of herself as a real marathoner while walking the entire distance. She wrote, "I have 2½ years of daily walking under my soles, to the tune of 2000-plus miles annually." She had walked marathons as cancer fund-raisers.

I wrote back, telling Cathy that our areas of agreement dwarfed any points of conflict. After that, we became regular correspondents, more so after signing on to email in the late nineties.

By then her approach to marathons had changed. "It was during the 1994 Los Angeles Marathon that I first saw Achilles Track Club members [with disabilities] and their companions. I then decided I wanted to be an Achilles companion. However, I noted that many were running; I was walking."

She couldn't have kept pace with them, so she started to run at age 48. Then came her fateful decision to sign up for a Jeff Galloway camp.

"With only six weeks of running to my credit," wrote Cathy, "I went off to my first camp experience with some trepidation. Would I be the oldest? Would I be the slowest? Although I was close on both counts, I was neither."

Jeff introduced her to the run/walk plan. "Somewhere along the way, I dubbed this 'intervals'," she recalled. "That fall I did my first interval marathon in 4:48." This put her about two hours ahead of walk-only pace.

Cathy Troisi became what her mentor now calls "the poster girl for Galloway Runwalkrun." Perhaps no one would stay true to this technique longer and more often.

She would complete more than 300 marathons and ultras (and still counting as of this writing). She also would qualify for Boston (*at* Boston while running in the charity division) with 4:00, on a run/walk minute mix of four and one.

Maybe she could have done all this by running steadily. But she wouldn't have wanted to try.

"The most I've ever run without intervals is six miles," Cathy once told me. "If I trained seriously, maybe I could run without the walking intervals. But that would make it seem like work, and I already have a job."

"I consider myself a recreational runner. I do my runs/walks mainly for fund-raising, and the same amount of money is raised whether I walk, run or 'interval'."

WATCH IT

By 1998 Cathy Troisi and I had arrived at the same place from opposite directions. She came to run/walk from walk-only, I from run-only. We now ran at similar pace and walked about the same amount.

By then she was more experienced with this practice, if only because she employed it more often. She taught me a new lesson – on how to refine my timing – when we ran/walked our first race together, if only how to refine my timing. Backstory is needed before I credit Cathy for her advice.

Ask me, "How far did you run today?" and my answer will be a wild guess. I don't know that number in miles and, outside of my rare races, don't care to know.

Ask me instead, "How *long* did you run?" and I'll tell you instantly and accurately. You see, I'm not a distance runner but a *time* runner. I run by minutes, not miles (for reasons noted later in this chapter).

My preference for time-running puts me in a small minority of runners. But by the 1990s new converts were arriving, via the newly popular walk breaks.

Stopping to walk for a certain short distance isn't practical, and often isn't even possible. Say you want to run a mile and then walk 100 yards. Mile-marking at races is spotty, and you'll never see another mark 100 yards later.

Plotting your training courses this way is too much work… especially since it's unnecessary. Easier by far is letting the watch plot the intervals.

Ask me how far I walk during the breaks, and I'll fumble for a conversion to an inexact distance. Ask how *long*, and you'll hear exact time – such as one minute.

My problem in 1998 was that checking those times required constant clock-watching. Cathy Troisi had already found a solution, a wristwatch that "talked."

69

DON'T LOOK NOW

I had a timing problem as walk breaks slipped more often into my runs. I'd spend as much time checking the next stopping and starting points on my watch as studying the passing scene and sifting my rambling thoughts. So often did I twist my wrist and neck for watch reading that they were at greater risk of overuse injuries than the feet and legs.

At the Around the Bay 30K in early 1998, I lined up beside Cathy Troisi at the start. I watched her set her watch and asked about it. "I've tried them all," she said, "and this is the best I've found."

It was a Timex Ironman Triathlon. "I can program it to beep at two different time intervals," said this committed walk-breaker. Here, she had set the watch to sound after four minutes of running, then again at the end of her one-minute walk. The watch automatically and continuously repeated.

"I never have to worry about the time," she added. "The watch does the thinking for me."

Cathy convinced me. The next week I went shopping for a beeping watch of my own, buying a low-end Ironman Triathlon model. The I.T. changed – no, revolutionized – my timing.

Most days I skipped over the stopwatch feature. Split-storage is irrelevant with distances unknown. Instead I put the watch in "timer" mode. This provides a repeating countdown from a pre-set starting point.

My standard cycle at the time was 10 minutes. After the first nine the watch signaled discreetly to start ticking off the one-minute break. (These counts could hide behind either the time-of-day or stopwatch reading, and go unseen while still sounding off as scheduled.)

The Timex now watched the time for me. It freed me to look and think beyond those numbers.

TIME PEACE

Time means a great deal to every runner. It means everything to me – more so than ever now that I'm a run/walker. Most days, miles don't count; only minutes do.

Once a stern taskmaster of mine, time has become a good friend. It used to taunt me with impossible deadlines to beat but now offers a satisfying quotas to meet.

Back when running with a reliable watch first became an option, I stepped into a time trap. Each course was measured, each run timed and each a course-record attempt.

The records fell easily at first. Dozens of seconds peeled away with every running of a course, and I could hardly wait for the next chance to improve.

Speed eventually neared its peak. The course records forced me to work ever harder to drop less and less time. These time trials came to feel like races, which are fun to run sporadically but not daily.

I began to fear the verdict of the watch while either losing the race against time that day or making the record even harder to break later. The time trap had snapped shut.

Arthur Lydiard offered an escape route. The coach from New Zealand reported in the mid-1960s than his runners, once known for their 100-mile weeks, often ignored mileage. They trained mostly by time periods, checking their pace for known distance only on special occasions.

Mile-counting stopped for me back then and has never resumed. I started running by time for practical reasons (a

71

way to keep records without having to measure a course and then to follow it as calibrated). I continued to run by the watch for better reasons.

The natural urge when running a distance is to push harder and finish sooner – to race against time. Every second beyond a self-imposed deadline is a little defeat.

When running to fill a time quota, however, the reverse happens. I can't make that time pass any faster by rushing, so I settle into a pace that feels right at the moment. Each minute above a quota is a little victory.

For these reasons the watch is my second most important piece of equipment, after shoes. Just as I'm always searching for the perfect shoe, I'm forever seeking the perfect watch (a quest described earlier in this chapter).

However, almost any digital stopwatch will cover the basics. All I really need is one that freezes time at the finish line.

That final time is important. It gives a comforting illusion of permanence not found in running by the mile. The hours, minutes and seconds stand as visible reminders that my effort put them all there. I preserve that time until the next day, when the watch lets my see how *impermanent* the efforts are.

If these watches had existed when I was still setting PRs (no, we weren't using sundials then, but most watches still had hands and went tick-tick), I might have retired the timepiece instead of erasing the hard-won numbers. The result would have stayed on the watch face until the batteries died.

But trying to make time stand still this way would have been a mistake. It is just as important to erase times eventually as to save them at first.

I savor time for a while, yes, but also pay special attention to clearing the watch. Pressing a button wipes out those precious, hard-earned numbers and replaces them with a line of zeros.

This act demonstrates graphically a turning away the past and moving ahead. Now's the time to put up new numbers that tell exactly the runner, or more likely the run/walker, I get to be today.

11. Talking Walking

(1999) TALK AMONG RUNNERS had never been easier, or quicker, than in the last years of the 20th century. The explosion of email made instant discussions possible. Each day I happily fielded dozens of these messages by 1999.

Two pet themes of mine converged in an email from Steve Vaughan, a subscriber to my monthly newsletter *Running Commentary*. He bought the ideas of taking walking breaks, and of running by time periods instead of distances.

He then said that I still had some explaining to do. He wanted to know, "Do you include walking breaks into total time for logging minutes?"

Put another way: Is it nobler to stop the watch during walking breaks or to let every minute count? This might seem a trivial concern, yet it still hounded me because it had to do with semantics. A word man, I asked myself: Is a run really a *run* if the walk time counts toward the day's total?

I once thought not and punched out with the first walking step, clocking in again only as the run resumed. It didn't feel quite right to say that I'd "run" an hour when it was really a run/*walk*. This offended my journalistic scruples, as did making up a word – "ralk"? "wun"? – to describe the mix.

Then I confessed in *Running Commentary* to an old habit of keeping walking minutes off the watch and out of the diary. The newsletter carried a whimsical piece about running 3:30 in a marathon – but needing 3:56 to finish it.

The extra time was spent walking.

This story brought howls of protest from several readers. They called this way of keeping score "cheating."

In fact, I never seriously claimed the lower time as official in that or any other race. But all training runs were by time periods, at unknown distances, and the walking minutes were kept off the watch.

Reaction to the newsletter piece made me question the honesty of this practice. Sufficiently shamed, I mended my record-keeping ways.

The minutes immediately began rolling on through the breaks, and into my diary went only the total run-plus-walk time. This practice continues today, with the watch starting at the first running step of the day and ending on the last. (Warmup and cooldown walks *don't* count.)

The breaks aren't running, to be sure. In the name of honesty and accuracy I take care to say I've "done" or "finished" a race or training session, not "run" it.

Yet the walks aren't time apart from the run but are an investment in it. They deserve full recognition for their contributions, and now receive it in my diary.

FREE TO DISAGREE

The walk-break idea isn't new, and isn't original with me. I'm simply a practitioner and promoter. But I do feel somewhat parental when critics spit out "walk" as if it's a disgusting word.

One 1999 article brought an unusual volume of email. I'd called the disagreement between purist runners and run/walkers "petty." A reader from Louisville, Jeff Stodghill, responded in the strongest terms:

"The issue of walkers in a marathon is not, as you refer

to it, 'petty.' (By the way, thanks for trivializing the opinions of those who happen to disagree with you.) A marathon is a race and a competition. I can't pole-vault 16 feet in accordance with the stated rules. Perhaps if I constructed a platform 12 feet up and started from there…"

A quieter argument came from a reader who requested anonymity: "I am not condoning elitism, but what is unfair about implementing and enforcing time limits for marathons? Be it six or seven hours, that is certainly long enough. All services stop, and a sweep bus is taken along the course to pick up those who did not make the cutoff. Many, many people I have seen strolling a marathon are simply not fit. They should be starting with shorter races such as 5K's and 10K's."

Diane Palmason, a world-class masters runner from Canada, sent this note: "Let everyone participate in whichever way they wish. One thought, though: I do wish there were some way that event organizers could do a better job of ensuring the people place themselves in the starting area in accordance with the pace at which they are most likely to proceed."

My reply to all three correspondents: I agree that run-walkers and walkers need educating on the etiquette of the road (line up correctly at the start, and don't impede runners as you walk)… that races have the right, even the duty as imposed by city officials, to set time limits on finishing… and that some people rush into marathons too quickly. I disagree that walkers are like pole-vaulters starting from a 12-foot platform. Walking usually slows our overall times, meaning we're like vaulters jumping from a hole several feet deep.

ONE FAST WALKER

We sat side by side for the first two days of the 1999 national track meet. This wasn't his assigned seat, and he had to move out as the stands grew more crowded. Besides, he had other business on the last day.

He wore a badge identifying him as an athlete, though he looked a little old for that. I asked his event.

"I'm in the 20-kilometer walk," he said. I didn't catch his name at first, but learned that he lived in Montana and worked as a college professor.

I've always liked race walkers. They have the same mindset as runners, train much the same way, and race at the same distances (or longer).

But I've never embraced their sport. It seems a little artificial to keep walking at speeds where the urge is to break into a run. It seems wrong to risk disqualification for going too fast.

I jokingly asked this race-walker, "If runners take walking breaks during their races, do walkers take running breaks?" He laughed and said, "Some try it, but they usually get caught and DQed."

I didn't see the championship 20K, contested outside the stadium early that Sunday. But I did see the victory ceremony. I learned that our companion from early in the meet was Jonathan Matthews and that he placed third.

At 43 he appeared to be the oldest athlete to make the 1999 World Championships team. Fast as he was, though, his time fell short of the qualifying standard.

I'd asked him earlier what pace he maintained for a 20K. "On a good day I'll do 6:50 to 6:55 per mile," he had said. "The best walkers in the world will go about 6:15s."

At this meet Jonathan walked exactly the pace he said

he could. Giving perspective, it's faster than I *ran* a 20K in all but my best years, far faster than I could have run that distance at age 43, and almost as fast a pace for 12.4 miles as I could have run a *single* mile in 1999.

These walkers *move*. The best of them go faster than all but about 10 percent of runners.

Thank you, Jonathan Matthews, for showing me that. Thanks for letting me know that you walkers are skilled athletes. And thanks for reminding me that the line between running and walking can be blurry.

It's especially blurred in a fast walk, which looks like running – and in a slow run, which looks like walking. So maybe it's time to stop splitting hairs over what's the acceptable and athletic way to cover long distances on foot.

WALKING LESSONS

My latest walking lessons arrived the same day in the late 1990s by postal (not e-) mail, one from the best possible source, the other a surprising one. The first correspondent was Ron Laird, who made four Olympic teams as a race-walker. The second was Richard Leutzinger, a man I'd always thought of as a pure runner.

Ron sent his book, *The Art of Fast Walking*. He addressed a chapter of the book, and a paragraph in his cover letter, to runners.

"For years," he told me, "I have felt it safer and more sensible for people to build their fitness with faster walking before attempting slower running training. We both know that race walking can get pretty crazy at the international level, with its rules and disqualifications. However, when slowed down to about twice the elite walkers' pace [12 minutes per mile or so], I feel that race-walking is the safest, healthiest and most convenient physical fitness activity ever invented."

Can't argue any of those points. Below seven minutes a mile most race "walkers" appear to the untrained eye to be running. But I'm sure that Ron's right that at a slower pace, where rules become irrelevant, the benefits are great and the risks small.

Richard Leutzinger surprised me by agreeing – at least with the general point of selective walking helping runners. We once shared the trails of Pebble Beach, California, but never ran together there because his pace was several gears above mine.

He was trained as a journalist. Though he now worked in health care, the urge to write stayed with him. He penned a book about baseball player Lefty O'Doul, then counted dozens of rejections before finding a publishing house to take the book.

Such endurance also served him well as a runner. In his late 50s he still ran marathons in the low-threes and contended for age-group prizes.

He wrote at the time, "I've run 52 marathons now and have never learned to drink on the run – probably because I've never tried. I've always felt that the time I lost while stopping to drink 5-6-7-8 times benefited me, so it wasn't time 'lost' at all. Those little walk breaks are really refreshing, physically and mentally.

"I determine whether I'm hydrated by whether I have to make any stops to pee, and whether my forehead feels dry or sweaty. If I'm well hydrated at 20 miles, I might consider passing up the last few drink stops – unless I just need that little break from running."

Richard also said he took breaks as long as 15 minutes in training, while indulging in his hobby of collecting stray golf balls on the Pebble Beach courses. This wrinkle in his routine hadn't hurt his racing.

"This fall I ran my fastest marathon in nearly four years," he said of his recent 3:15. "So I guess the system works okay."

12. Long Walks

(2000) RUN/WALK isn't a refuge for the undertrained, untalented and unmotivated. I remind naysayers that the man who most shaped my thoughts on this practice was Tom Osler, an ultrarunner. No one could question his fitness, ability and dedication, or that of any runner featured in this chapter. They've all run very long, and fast, and yet aren't too proud to walk as needed.

Jeff Hagen, a dentist by profession, won five ultras in 1998, at age 51. He backed up his deeds with words in a article for *Marathon & Beyond* magazine, which told about his way of walking in races.

His subject was 24-hour races, where he walked for longer periods than the minute-at-a-time that Jeff Galloway and others generally recommend. Hagen's strategy arose from tips he once picked up in a mountaineering class.

"One of these principles held that taking frequent rest breaks of three to five minutes each was more efficient and effective than taking shorter or longer breaks," he wrote in *M&B*. "I was taught that less than three minutes did not provide adequate rest, while more than five minutes resulted in little additional benefit and wasted valuable time.

"Applying this to walking breaks [during a long run] suggests that breaks of a minute or less may not be as effective as those in the three- to five-minute range. This concept has been reported in running research literature."

I don't know if this qualifies as research, but I looked back at the writings of a godfather of walk breaks. Tom

Osler, a mathematics professor, was a top ultrarunner a generation earlier. His *Serious Runner's Handbook*, published in 1978, underlined his own five-minute recommendation.

Osler's old way of walking, and Jeff Hagen's endorsement of it, rates another look from runners whose marathons are their "ultras."

WALK OF AGES

To walk is to surrender? Two good old friends of mine could argue that point, but let's have their efforts speak for them. Their average age was nearly 80 when I wrote this column about them:

A runner's great fear came true for Ted Corbitt. He found in the 1970s that his asthma made running intolerable.

This loss could have devastated Ted, an Olympic marathoner in his youth and later a renowned ultrarunner. He could have descended from high activity to none.

Instead he transitioned smoothly into walking. Not strolling through his New York City neighborhood but a different way of traveling the big miles that he'd long covered.

For example, he averaged 50½ miles per day in a six-day race named for him. In 2001 he wrote to me about his walks as his 83rd birthday approached.

"Since I stopped running, I sometimes walk around Manhattan Island, which is 31-plus miles by the route I take. I've probably run or walked this more than 100 times.

"In fact, I had planned to walk it the day of the terrorist attacks – and would have passed the site of the World Trade Center after its collapse. Of course I changed my plans. I decided to walk another 30-mile course, going up the Hudson River and back."

Ted added that "most of my walks are 10-milers." Running or walking, he remains a beacon for aging actively.

John Keston became, at 69-plus, the oldest marathoner to break three hours. At 71 he ran the then-fastest time (3:00:58) for anyone past his 70th birthday.

The record-breaking abruptly stopped for John when he fractured a hip in a bicycling crash. Soon after that injury healed, he broke a foot while building his own home.

Both times John returned to running. But he went several years between marathons. The professional stage performer was relegated to singing the National Anthem at races.

At the 2001 Portland Marathon, he doubled. After his solo performance of the Star-Spangled Banner, he stepped in among the runners.

John ran 3:22:59 that day. At two months shy of his 77th birthday he became the oldest runner to break 3½ hours.

This was a test of his then-new training method, which had led to a summer of age-group record-breaking at shorter distances. For half of his mileage, John walked. He didn't mix walk breaks into his runs but mixed walk and running *days*.

"I predicated the concept of this kind of training that body-builders use," he said. "They base their approach on the premise of never working the same muscle more than every third day. I figured that I could save my running muscles by just walking two days in a row (usually five to six miles each day) and then running long (typically 14 to 17 miles) on the third day."

83

John added, "I'd like to see this system tried on some younger runners, since I believe that most youngsters overtrain." Oldsters too.

TWO TOURISTS

Seeing them here, strolling toward the beach on the Big Island of Hawaii, you'd think they were just two more old tourists. These two walkers were friends and longtime running-mates from California. They were much more than tourists, and theirs wasn't a simple stroll to the beach.

Paul Reese was in Hawaii in late 1997 to finish what no one had done before. At age 80 he would become the first runner to cross all 50 states on foot.

He simply walked now – at the end of the seven-year, 7600-mile odyssey – so he could share this last lap with Ralph Paffenbarger. "Paff," then 75, was a world-renowned medical researcher and himself a runner of note before a heart condition eased him down to walking pace.

Paul wrote in his book *The Old Man and the Road*, "Paff and I have run 1200 miles alongside each other in races – including such famous ones as the Comrades (90-kilometer) Marathon in South Africa, the London Marathon and about 10 Honolulu Marathons. I was his pit-crew captain when at age 61 he set a 60-plus record of 22:03 for the Western States 100-Mile Endurance Run.

"But that was then – prior to his heart attack and subsequent operation. And this is now – when Paff is limited to walking and, I suspect, grateful to be alive and capable of that."

Paff's heart problems were first detected in 1991. He underwent surgery three years later, and its complications included three cardiac arrests.

"All told I was in the hospital five weeks," he said in Paul's book. "After that my recovery was slow. It was six months before I was able to do daily walks of three miles."

Through it all his medical work continued. This was the same Dr. Ralph Paffenbarger, epidemiologist, who had studied the health habits of Harvard alumni. He had gathered the best evidence yet that exercise promotes longevity, and still traveled the world speaking about his findings.

Paul himself had traveled heavily in 1997 with his wife Elaine and their two Labradors, Rebel and Brudder. Hawaii was the 23rd and last state crossing of the year.

He too had reason to feel grateful for coming this far. All of the cross-state running has come after his successful treatment for prostate cancer.

"Each of us," he said of his and Paff's last day in Hawaii, "was grateful just to be alive, to be active, to be fully functional physically and mentally. Once again I marveled at how such a simple act – doing this walking with a close friend – could overflow my day with joy. Who needs drugs?"

Two strolling tourists, yes – and much more. These two, even more than other elders, were walking history books. Look past their well-worn covers and you'd see the wealth of experience that brought them to this place and time.

REESE'S PIECES

The most remarkable thing about Paul Reese's earlier run across the United States was what he *didn't* do. He didn't try raise any money. He didn't act as a paid spokesman for seniors or cancer patients. He didn't run to draw attention

85

to himself.

Paul kept his intentions quiet partly to protect himself from doubters who would have said, "It can't be done at your age," and from friends who might have said, "It shouldn't be done in your health."

The Auburn, California, runner would turn 73 the week his journey of national and personal discovery was to begin, in 1990. An article of faith in this sport is that recovery from big efforts slows down with age. Yet he planned to run a marathon a day for four straight months.

Paul also was coming off a health scare. A cancerous prostate had been diagnosed three years earlier, and apparently had been treated successfully with radiation. But what chain reactions might the stress of this run set off?

So he plotted the journey quietly. He organized it without sponsorship, without a support crew other than his wife Elaine and without seeking any publicity. He didn't even tell me, a longtime friend but also a journalist and natural-born gossip.

I didn't learn what he was doing until he'd already done it. San Francisco newspaper columnist Herb Caen wrote on August 21st, 1990, "Tomorrow 73-year-old Paul Reese of Auburn will become the oldest man ever to run across the United States. He started April 21st, knee deep in the Pacific Ocean near Jenner [California], and finishes in the Atlantic at Hilton Head, South Carolina."

Paul had averaged his marathon a day for 124 straight days, totaling 3192 miles. He told me later, "I never ran one of those 'marathons' straight through. Instead I ran a few miles, stopped for a snack and chat with Elaine, then ran a few more to the next pitstop. Most days I was on the road twice as long as I would have taken to finish a standard marathon."

Each night he captured thoughts and observations from his hours on the back roads of America. He meant this only as a personal memory book.

"I wanted it to record the heat of battle, and not write it later and have actuality changed by reflection," he told me. He sent me his manuscript with the warning, "Just don't advertise it. I don't want to get in the book-supply business."

A copy somehow found its way to people who *are* in the business of supplying books. WRS Publishing took serious interest in releasing a slimmer version of his 800-page journal. The resulting book, T*en Million Steps*, retained all of the immediacy and intimacy of the diary form.

"People have missed the whole point if they see this book as a jock thing," Paul wrote. "I'm not saying, 'Look at me – Mr. Genes, Mr. Macho'."

He also wasn't saying, "Boy, look at me! I had cancer, and I'm a tiger now. The early detection is a tribute to modern medicine, not running."

So why did Paul Reese go this far? For the "enjoyment, enjoyment like the pioneers who walked, rode a horse or traveled by wagon across the country. Enjoyment of lessons learned from studying first-hand the varied geography and people of our country. Enjoyment with Elaine in injecting some adventure and variety into our lives, in departing from routine and in together meeting a somewhat difficult challenge. And, yes, the sheer enjoyment and deep gratitude of being mobile at my vintage."

13. Accidental Marathon

(2008) THE WALK BREAK will only take you so far. It won't carry you through to the end of a marathon unless you also train for it – not, anyway, without walking more than running the late miles, and not without walking because you choose but because you must. This I learned in 2000, the year of my only unplanned and untrained-for marathon.

I'd often written that you can't fake a marathon. Maybe you can run a 10K without training for it, but not a marathon. My problem was remembering my own advice. Memory failed me in midrun at the 2000 Napa Valley Marathon.

I'd gone there without thinking of going anywhere near that far. I wasn't ready, having run nothing long since a half-marathon race almost two months earlier.

My thought was to run the first 10 miles with Jan Seeley, the publisher of *Marathon & Beyond*. Rich Benyo, *M&B's* editor, co-directed Napa Valley. He insisted I wear a race number even if not planning to finish.

The sport's great thinker George Sheehan once said, "When you pin on a number, you pledge to do your best." I didn't consciously take this oath but now wore the evidence of having done so.

At 10 miles I told Jan, "I'll do a few more." At 13, "I'll keep going as long as you do."

Jan was going 16 miles that day as training for a later marathon, and she stuck to that plan. As she stopped, I told her, "I'll go a little farther and then catch a ride."

Two more miles down the road, no ride could be found. I was told, "You can wait for the sag wagon, but it could be another hour before the last runner gets here."

Rain had started to fall. Running mixed with walking seemed a better choice than standing and waiting.

A normal blend of run/walk had taken me this far, but now I'd done about all that my limited training would allow. The new mix became walks mixed with brief runs.

I finished, but it wasn't pretty, then or later. Another truism of marathoning: The less you train before, the more you suffer during and after. My hurting was mild on race day compared to the after-effects that struck later.

MARATHON FEVER

At first I thought that the accidental marathon at Napa Valley had let me off easily. Post-race pains were no worse or longer-lasting than if I'd trained right, maybe because I'd run so slowly and walked so much.

Normal running soon resumed, probably too soon. Long after the soreness was gone, the tiredness persisted.

My defenses stayed down, so low that they couldn't repel a mysterious illness. Its symptoms were flu-like – low-grade fever, persistent cough, heavy fatigue – and they hung on for two full months.

I ran almost nothing for those months, walked little, and began to worry that I'd never feel better. Just getting from one end of the day to the other was a "marathon."

My doctor never identified that illness. The best he could do was rule out the worst possibilities.

The long-lasting fever finally cooled. More months passed as I inched back toward normal runs. You appreciate even those little ones all the more after you've lost them for a while.

After recovering fully, I still avoided making the efforts that racing required, fearing pushing my immune system too far again. Only a few times each year was my distance longer than short or my pace faster than comfortable.

I still went to races, but now mostly to watch other runners. "Why aren't you running?" they would ask.

Two answers. The first, "I forgot to train," usually drew a laugh. The second, "I like to run too much to race," brought a look of bewilderment, as if I were speaking poorly translated Swahili.

Here's a clearer translation: Daily runs meant much more to me than races, if only because the normal days outnumbered the race days by more than a hundred to one. If racing jeopardized my normal running, as it did after Napa 2000, the race was not worth the risk.

A BREAK FROM WALKS

In the years immediately after this illness episode, I wrote and spoke more and more about walk breaks. This while taking fewer and fewer myself. A column from 2002 tells why:

Some of my best friends are run/walkers. I know hundreds of people who swear by the breaks, saying they couldn't (or wouldn't) finish marathons without them.

I've walked intentionally in every one of my marathons since 1980 – about a dozen in all. I've stopped to walk during every long run in those years. I've beaten the drum for this practice in writing and speaking for decades.

But now comes a confession: I don't do much walking these days. Does this mean I've crossed over to the other side in the great debate, joining the run-only purists? Does this make me a liar in print and a traitor to my walking friends?

No, I haven't parted ways philosophically with my "second brother" Jeff Galloway. I don't say that any of his devotees are wrong.

Recently I wrote again in praise of walking, this for two chapters in the book *Fitness Running* (written with Dr. Richard Brown). One targeted people breaking into running. The other advised runners recovering from injuries.

I don't say I'll never walk again. If long runs – by my definition, any lasting longer than an hour – return to my routine, I won't hesitate to restore the breaks. If I try another marathon, I'll again lean heavily on the walks. And if in a weak moment I'm tempted back into fast interval training, I'll walk the recovery laps.

But for what I'm doing now, I don't need to or want to walk. The switch came, as many of my changes do, without warning or forethought.

This was a snap decision to simplify my running. I would run about the same amount each day, and would simply run the whole way.

First change: over several months the length of runs nearly doubled (which sounds a little more impressive than saying that each one was a few miles longer). Second change: overnight the walk breaks disappeared.

One day I walked, the next day not. The rationale came later: I wanted to feel more like a runner. The best way to do this was to spend all my allotted time actually running.

I'm running slower than ever, but this pace seems to grant many of the same injury-protective benefits as walk breaks. If I need to bail some days, that's it. I take the ultimate walk break – all the way back home.

Nowadays I plan walks only as a brief warmup and cooldown, and as the preferred substitute activity on my weekly non-run day. The only midrun breaks are unplanned – while waiting for traffic to pass, or for my dog Buzz to drink, water a bush or fertilize a field. And these aren't walks but stops.

MY "LAST" MARATHON

I'd raced enough for anyone's lifetime, more than 700 times. What was left to prove? Well, there was one thing.

Was it to prove that the training program prescribed to the Marathon Teams, which I began coaching in 2005, and in my *Marathon Training* book was good enough to use myself? Not really. I already knew that from many earlier go-rounds.

The answer that came closer to the truth than any other was that I didn't want that accidental marathon in 2000 to stand forever as my last. "Latest" was a better word for it.

Before too much more time passed, I needed to correct my Napa Valley mistakes – in training, planning, pacing, recovery. Maybe I wouldn't go out in style (when had the late miles of my marathons ever been less than a struggle?). But I wanted to walk away proud of having done this one as right as I knew how.

Napa Valley seemed the perfect place for this one, where I could correct old mistakes made there. This was perfect time, my 50th anniversary of running races.

By then I'd coached the Marathon Team for several years. Those runners would ask, "When are you going to do another one yourself?" What they really wanted to know: Did I believe enough in the program that I gave them to follow it myself?

I did, and I would. My training started, as theirs always did, four months before the race. Like theirs, it climbed from a first long day of just seven miles to a peak of 21 miles.

The only difference between the team's training and mine was the walking. Theirs was optional, and seldom adopted. For me these breaks were essential. I stuck with cycles of run four minutes and walk one throughout the mileage buildup, and planned to run/walk the same way on race day.

That day went perfectly. I never needed to run less or walk more than 4/1. The pace, though slow, never slumped. Recovery would be uncomplicated.

My time was neither notable nor shameful. You could look it up on the Napa Valley Marathon's website or MarathonGuide.com, so I'll save you the trouble. It was 5:11:02.

A friend asked at the finish line, "Does it embarrass you not to break five hours?" It wasn't a harsh question. He knew I'd once run sub-three, he knew that I'm a little more visible than most five-hour marathoners, and he was concerned about my feelings at that moment.

No, I told him, this time carries no shame. If slowing down bothered me, I would have stopped running marathons after the first few. Or I would have chosen one now where no one knew me, then run in disguise under an assumed name.

If indeed Napa had been my last marathon, it completed

perfect bookends at this distance: the fastest one at the start and the slowest at the end, with more than 40 years and two-plus hours standing between those times.

If this marathon happened to be my last, I could shrug and say I'd had my turn. I'd run good times and *had* even better ones. Now I could focus fully on giving that chance to others, as a guide who had gone the way they wanted to go.

14. Walking Away

(2009) CHECKING INTO a hotel before my first marathon since starting to coach marathoners, I'd been handed an oversized greeting card. It read, "Since we can't be here in body, we're here in spirit." It was signed by all of my Eugene marathoners.

A column I'd posted on my website at a dark hour of marathon morning was addressed to coaches. It ended, "Teach by example. Ask your runners to do no training or racing that you wouldn't do (and haven't done, or are doing) yourself."

I did that training and finished my race. Back home the next day, I resumed my role of standing and watching, handing drinks to and cheering for our runners as they reached 15 miles in training. After walking stiffly to their starting line, I told them, "I can teach you to walk this way the day after your marathon."

They laughed politely at this line, most of them knowing already how tough walking would be the next day. However, I'd had little success teaching them to walk during their runs. I was happy if they just paused at drink stations to get the liquids *in* instead of *on* themselves.

By now I also taught a running class at the University of Oregon. One student there refused to walk, ever. She ran the recoveries during interval training and ran to cool down, when everyone else walked. She hadn't yet noticed that walking speeds up the recovery.

A runner from the Marathon Team announced that one of her goals in the race was "not to walk a step." She didn't succeed that way, and as a result couldn't give herself full credit for PRing. She didn't notice that most of the runners around her did some walking, if only through the drink stations.

The student reminded me of myself at her age, not yet 20. The marathoner reflected myself at that same early stage of marathon life. Back then, I too never walked by choice. I not only ran my interval recoveries and grabbed drinks on the run; I also avoided walking anywhere, anytime.

I'd long since made peace with walking. But very few of the runners I taught and coached had yet recognized its beauties and benefits. I didn't insist that they run/walk my way, only telling them this practice was available if they ever wanted to try it.

TEAMWORK

We never trained together, the Marathon Team and I. This was partly because our paces didn't match, but mostly because my job was to support them all, not to run with one or none. I was old enough to be their father, if not their granddad. We were going different ways, they getting faster, I slower; they resisting walking, I embracing it.

Yet I'd never felt closer to a group of runners since high school almost a half-century earlier, when I served as student assistant coach my senior year. Then, I ran well ahead of my teammates; now, I would have trailed far behind most of them. Didn't matter; we stayed close in other ways.

Finally, in 2009, after watching hundreds of these runners finish marathons, I entered one with them. A full team would join me at Napa Valley, where I'd gone alone

96

the year before.

In the intervening year I'd completed another "marathon" or sorts in that year, a medical one. It had gone smoothly and ended well, so I expected no less the next time.

This was to be my graduation celebration from a marathon of daily radiation treatments for prostate cancer. They'd stretched from Halloween to the first workday of the new year. In January 2009 we (and I say "we" because any cancer involves more than the individual) still didn't know how well this therapy had worked.

The odds were favorable, according to my radiologist. "Nationally the success rate with this type of treatment for your stage of the disease is close to 90 percent," he said. "My numbers are even higher."

While weighing the treatment options, I had talked with Elaine Reese, whose late husband Paul had chosen radiation and lived actively and cancer-free for nearly two more decades. "It went well for him," said Elaine. "He never missed a run during those daily sessions."

Paul's story convinced me to choose radiation, which has improved vastly since Paul's diagnosis in 1988. Running each of my 45 treatment days was one of several goals (or at least hopes). The others were: no medical appointment unkept, no coaching session unattended, no writing deadline unmet, no diary page unfilled. I met every goal.

This wasn't heroic, or foolish. If pushing on had been a struggle, I would have cut back immediately. Life went on as before because it could. The radiation was non-invasive to both body and normal routines.

My running during treatment wasn't the same as before. In some ways it was better. Marathon training passed without a hitch (a rarity at my age), and it included my longest training day ever (in time, not distance). The only concession to my treatments was upping the walk breaks from one to two minutes after each four-minute run.

I reserved number 45 to wear on race day at Napa Valley, a nod to the number of radiation zappings. I looked forward to running for the first time with (behind, anyway) the Marathon Team that I coached. Before, I'd always stood waiting for these runners from first to last. Now I would be the last, and hoped without asking that many of them would stick around after their finish to watch mine.

Only during the taper did these plans unravel. For many runners this is the worst part of the program. It's too late to gain more from training, but not too late to blow it all with an ill-timed medical mishap.

Every little symptom expands in the mind to threaten your marathon. The scratchiness in your throat is surely strep. The ache in your ankle must be a stress fracture.

I've had every possible symptom before marathons. Some were imaginary, all were exaggerated in the worried mind. I'd always started a marathon with something wrong, but never had it kept me from starting. The healing power of a starter's gun had always amazed me.

An injury struck two weeks before marathon day, during the taper. I made a dumb mistake by lifting too much (ironically it was the training team's loaded drink cooler), with bad form (too much arms, not enough legs) and without help (offered but waved off). My lower back instantly let me know the errors of my ways.

The pain was real. But I assumed that it wasn't as serious as it seemed to my pre-marathon mind. It was. Two days before Napa Valley, after hurting every step in a run just one-tenth the race distance, I made a hard decision:

Don't risk it. This is no way to start a marathon, let alone try to finish one.

Maybe I could have walked all the way from Calistoga to Napa, but I didn't try. As a slow walker I would have missed Napa Valley's six-hour cutoff time by a wide margin.

But that would have been a minor miss compared to losing sight of the 18 runners I'd coached all winter and had talked into coming here. There could be other marathon opportunities for me, but never would I have another chance to see each of these teammates finish this one.

MOVING FORWARD

I'm half the runner in the 2010s that I was in the 1960s. I run half as much now, and each mile takes twice as long as it did at my fastest. I'm okay with all that, as long as I keep moving forward somehow.

Everyday activity is a habit I never want to break. But now I walk almost as much as I run on "run" days, and take more walk-only days. As the gap between running and walking pace shrinks, the line between the two activities blurs.

I never had any problem being known as a run/walker. I first outed myself as one, at races and in writing, in the 1970s. Coming to terms with my slowdown took much longer.

Like most runners I'm a numbers nerd. I might not remember breakfast this morning, but my recall of race times from as far back as 1958 is instant and usually accurate. What was exciting when my times were improving became haunting once the last PR was set (in 1979).

I could see ever more clearly how far short of my old self my current one fell. My fastest mile time was 4:18, while now I'd be lucky to run a *half*-mile that fast. My last marathon's pace was perilously close to double that of my best average of 6:30 miles.

My fast past continued to haunt me until a simple realization struck while writing this book. It wasn't the most obvious fact: that my age has tripled since those PR years. No, I finally recognized that what I'd done then and do now are incomparable activities, with different ways of keeping score.

Then, I ran to see how fast I could race, in minutes and seconds trimmed from my times. But my serious racing ended in the early 1980s. Comparing paces, current versus past, is a no-win exercise.

Now, the best measure of success doesn't appear on the watch, in times beaten. It's on the calendar, in months and years of steady activity added. I suspect that slowing down and embracing walking has kept me moving forward this long. I know for sure that slow running beats no running, and walking beats stopping.

At this writing, in late 2012, I am pushing 70 (and may be pulling it as you read these lines). Four years after my last marathon finish, I've yet to try for another.

Those same four years have raced past since my diagnosis of prostate cancer. Treatment was successful, with all follow-up tests so far coming back clean. But these came at a cost. Hormonal changes led to low energy, which led to less running, which led to weight gain, which led to slower and shorter runs, and to more walks.

More days are walk-only, which I don't hesitate to take when soreness or fatigue dictate. Better not to run for a day or few than risk weeks or months off with a big injury or illness.

Yet full rest days are quite rare. Even when purely walking I go out at the same time and for the same amount of time, to the same places, in the same shoes and clothes. I love the everyday routine – being outside in the early morning air with feet meeting earth – as much as how quickly or slowly I'm moving there.

15. Old Man Walking

(2015) AS THE YEARS have added up, my public roles in running have shrunk. At 60, I ran my last true race; at 61, I quit going on the road once or twice a month as a speaker; at 64, I ran/walked my last marathon; at 68, I wrote my last column for a national running magazine.

I didn't become anti-social or reclusive, exactly, and didn't fully retire from running, writing or speaking. But I now enjoy relative anonymity after being too public a figure in this sport for too long.

I run (and increasingly, walk) alone. I write mainly for an audience of one (myself). I speak mostly to my training teams (and then only briefly).

If I'm known at all in my hometown beyond these small groups of runners, it's for another role played in recent years. That's as a local poster boy for a cause near to my heart (and points south): prostate cancer awareness.

At age 65, as you've read, I was diagnosed with prostate cancer. I've put modesty and privacy aside and spoken out about my condition, in hopes of helping other men avoid or treat it.

I made PSAs (public service announcements) on television for PSA (prostate specific antigen) testing. These appeared so often that strangers sometimes told me, "I saw you in that ad."

I'm the designated greeter at the Prost8K, a clever name for a race that benefits a great cause: a free screening program. I first attended a support group to be supported; later I went there to give support to the newly diagnosed.

My cancer was sent into deep remission, if not entirely cured. But I didn't escape it without some cost, which I gladly paid.

Hormone suppression figured into the early treatment. It added pounds to my waistline and minutes to my running pace. I've never lost the former or gained back the latter.

This combination gradually reduced my running range. I couldn't run as far as I still wanted to go, so I evolved over the next few years from a runner taking a few walk breaks to a walker who ran a little.

For the first five years post-treatment, I joined a Relay for Life, the cancer fund-raiser usually held on a track. The first three were traditional run-walks.

I celebrated the fourth year differently. My first-ever hamstring tear (a "speed" injury at a time when I'd never been slower) temporarily ended all running. This happened right before the 2012 Relay, which led to another first: walking an organized event, the whole four hours.

Never had a walk lasted longer for me. I didn't know exactly what my old walk-only high was, but only that this new one wouldn't long remain my lifetime high.

That "PR" lasted only a year. The fifth cancer-versary (the traditional time for pronouncing a patient "cured") brought a five-hour walk at the Relay... and a vow to extend to a marathon in the sixth year.

All previous celebrations had been unpublicized and unaccompanied by anyone who knew what I was doing. The marathon was different.

At age 70, I entered an official one – the 2014 Yakima River Canyon Marathon in Washington, which offered a generous early start for slowpokes like me who mainly walked. And I accepted help from a few young runners on my training team.

Laurel Mathiesen, Sara Tepfer and Jesse Centeno made the 600-mile round trip on their own. Then they ran until they'd made up my two-hour head start.

From 22 miles on, we walked in together. We finished, in 6½ hours on the early-start clock, and my first written comments afterward still stand as the most accurate:

"Walking a marathon is very different from running one; much less intense, for one thing. But it isn't easy with its extra hours. Laurel, Sara and Jesse made the hard final miles go better, and they made this day four times more rewarding than it would have been as a private effort."

TEAMING AT NEWPORT

This experience encouraged an encore the next year, my seventh post-diagnosis, this time at the 2015 Newport (Oregon) Marathon. Runners from the team walked with me again, and others waited at the finish. I thank them for this support – and their patience.

Fittingly for the personal anniversary being marked that week, this marathon took me nearly seven hours. But that clocking was incidental to another bigger, better number.

This event celebrated 10 years for my training team, whose first race also had been at Newport. I am quietly proud to have gone these miles, here and for the past decade. And I am loudly proud to have shared so much with so many teammates.

Teammates Laurel Mathiesen and Sara Tepfer stayed with me to the end of this marathon walk. (Jesse Centeno photo)

98792196R10059

Made in the USA
Columbia, SC
03 July 2018